the
end
of
me

What people are saying about …

The End of Me

"A wise, mature person is known for his understanding. The more pleasant his words, the more persuasive he is. Kyle Idleman is one of today's great young teachers. He's a brilliant, compassionate, and thoughtful communicator who presents the truth of Scripture in a fresh, relevant, and persuasive way."

Rick Warren, author of *The Purpose-Driven Life*

Praise for …

AHA

"Kyle knows where we live and where we could live with God's help. He is committed to helping us move in the right direction. If you need a helping hand in your journey, he'll point you to the right Person."

Max Lucado, pastor of Oak Hills
Church and author of *Grace*

"Kyle will challenge you to grow from a fair-weather fan to a full-time follower of Christ."

Craig Groeschel, senior pastor of
LifeChurch.tv and author of *Fight*

"Kyle will challenge even the most obedient Christians to relook at their relationship with Christ."

Mike Huckabee, former governor of
Arkansas and bestselling author

"Like his preaching, Kyle's writings will bring you face-to-face with areas you need to change and the One who has the power to change you."

Dave Stone, senior pastor of Southeast
Christian Church and author of
Raising Your Kids to Love the Lord

"Fresh, insightful, practical—Kyle's writing and teaching are helping countless people. I'm thrilled with how God is using him to challenge and encourage both Christians and those who are checking out the faith. Count me among his many fans!"

Lee Strobel, bestselling author and
professor at Houston Baptist University

the
end
of
me

**Where Real Life in
the Upside-Down
Ways of Jesus Begins**

kyle idleman

David Ⓒ Cook®
transforming lives together

THE END OF ME
Published by David C Cook
4050 Lee Vance View
Colorado Springs, CO 80918 U.S.A.

David C Cook Distribution Canada
55 Woodslee Avenue, Paris, Ontario, Canada N3L 3E5

David C Cook U.K., Kingsway Communications
Eastbourne, East Sussex BN23 6NT, England

The graphic circle C logo is a registered trademark of David C Cook.

Unless otherwise noted, all Scripture quotations are taken from the Holy
Bible, New International Version®, NIV®. Copyright © 1973, 2011 by
Biblica, Inc.® Used by permission of Zondervan. All rights reserved worldwide.
www.zondervan.com. Scripture quotations marked NCV are taken from the
New Century Version®. Copyright © 2005 by Thomas Nelson, Inc. Used by
permission. All rights reserved; NLT are taken from the *Holy Bible*, New Living
Translation, copyright © 1996, 2007 by Tyndale House Foundation. Used by
permission of Tyndale House Publishers, Inc., Carol Stream, Illinois 60188. All
rights reserved; MSG are taken from *THE MESSAGE*. Copyright © by Eugene
H. Peterson 1993, 2002. Used by permission of NavPress Publishing Group.

LCCN 2015933705
ISBN 978-1-4347-0707-9
eISBN 978-0-7814-1363-3

© 2015 Kyle Idleman
Published in association with the literary agency of
The Gates Group, www.the-gates-group.com.

The Team: Alex Field, Ingrid Beck, Alice Crider, Amy
Konyndyk, Tiffany Thomas, Karen Athen
Cover Design: Faceout Studio, Jeff Miller

Printed in the United States of America
First Edition 2015

1 2 3 4 5 6 7 8 9 10

073015

To Dave Stone, Tony Young, and Don Gates.
I am honored and humbled to partner with
each of you in making known the mysteries
of the gospel. Your service and sacrifice in
advancing the kingdom inspire me.

Contents

Introduction

I sat in my church office staring at a blank screen, preparing to write this introduction, when my assistant reminded me of a few phone calls I needed to make. I decided to knock out the phone calls before I started to type.

The first call went to voice mail, and I left a message. The next one wouldn't be so easy. I was returning a call to a man named Brian. I read in my notes that his eighteen-month-old son had died a few weeks earlier. I didn't know the details, but as a father of four, I can't imagine such loss. I said a prayer as I dialed his number. Brian answered with a monotone "Hello." Having had many conversations like this over the past twenty years, I knew there was not much I could say. So, after expressing my heartbreak for his loss, I allowed silence to settle into our conversation. After a few moments, Brian spoke four words that I was not prepared for.

"I backed over him."

More silence as his words sank in.

I then told him I had not been made aware of that and asked him if he wanted to tell me what happened. He went on to explain that they didn't know their son had walked outside. In fact, they didn't even know he was capable of opening the door to go outside.

Listening, I found myself wondering how parents survive such tragedy. When he finished telling me what they had been going through, I followed up by asking a question that always feels ridiculous in moments like this: "How are you?"

Believe me, I know that doesn't seem like the right question to ask. What's he supposed to say? And yet I knew he was calling weeks after it happened for a reason. I assumed he had something in mind to share with me. After describing his horrific experience, he began to convey how he discovered Jesus in a way he never had before. His faith had gone from attending church once in a while—as tradition—to running into God's arms in complete desperation. I had a page open on my computer where I was going to be writing the introduction for this book, and without even thinking about it, I quickly typed out something he said:

"I feel like I reached this point in my life when I had absolutely nothing left, and it turns out that for the first time in my life, Jesus has become real. Do you know what I mean? Is that unusual?"

Yes, I know what you mean. No, it's not unusual.

When he reached the end of himself, he discovered Jesus. I prayed for Brian and his family, then hung up and wondered how many other people would say they experienced this same kind of beautiful irony. I jumped on Facebook and posted the following:

Finish this sentence: Jesus became real when …

Within a few hours I received hundreds of responses. Some of them were general:

- I could no longer pretend that I was in control.
- I had to admit that I couldn't fix things.
- I knew I wasn't strong enough.
- I had no one else to turn to.
- I had disappointed everyone who loved me.

Most of the responses were specific:

- I was told I had three months to live because of stage IV cancer.
- I found out my husband was having an affair, and I never felt more alone in my life.
- I sat on my bed with my dad's gun in my hand but said a prayer before pulling the trigger. I don't remember the last time I had prayed.
- It became clear that I had lost control of my addiction.
- The divorce papers arrived in the mail, and I could no longer pretend I could fix things.
- Jesus reached into one of the darkest places on earth, a strip club, to show me he loved me. I realized there was no place he couldn't find me.
- My depression became too much for me to bear.
- I was forced out of my thirty-year job and had no idea what I was going to do.
- I was pregnant, my kidneys were failing, and the doctors told me to abort. I prayed for the

first time in a long time. My daughter is now twenty-three.

- I finally admitted I wasn't strong enough to save my marriage or end my addiction to porn.
- My husband was killed in a car accident.
- The ultrasound said the baby's heart had stopped beating.

And then I read the one response that seemed to capture them all. In one way or another, what Brian and all my Facebook friends were expressing could be wrapped up in this single response:

Jesus became real when … I came to the end of me.

Even though most of us can point to a significant event like the ones above, getting to "the end of me" is not just one moment in life. Reaching the end of me is a daily journey I must make because it's where Jesus shows up and my real life in him begins.

Getting to the end of me is not an easy journey, because me doesn't want to go there. Me doesn't like confrontation, and me is most interested in the promotion and success of me. Me would much prefer to read a book about advancing me, not ending me. But Jesus said in Luke 9 that whoever wants to hang on to his life will lose it, but whoever loses his life will find it. He said a lot of seemingly upside-down things like that.

I've come to realize that if me gets his way, I'll miss out on the real life I'm meant to live. The life in which I love others and make a difference in the world.

Isn't that the life you really want too? If so, I invite you to join me in looking at the upside-down, paradoxical teachings of Jesus that will help you get good at reaching the end of your own me.

Why would I want to get to the end of me? you might ask. Because I'm guessing, like me, you want more than worldly success in this life. You want more than a few fleeting moments of happiness.

You want to …

… love and be loved.

… make a difference in the world.

… leave well.

In the first section of this book, we will focus on four of the beatitudes from the Sermon on the Mount. These specific beatitudes will help lead us, sometimes kicking and screaming, down this path to real life. I want to warn you now that so much of Jesus's teachings seem oppositional to what we have come to accept. And the life he invites us to is not just countercultural; it's counterintuitive. More often than not it flies in the face of what feels right. Each chapter will focus on a different paradoxical teaching of Christ. Jesus will show us that blessings begin and fulfillment is found in the least likely place—the end of ourselves.

In the second section of this book, we will see that when we get to the end of ourselves and finally realize we aren't strong enough, smart enough, or talented enough, then ironically we are in the best position to be used by God in significant ways.

Real life is found at the end of me. As you read this book, I am praying that Jesus will take you on a path to the end of you—and straight into your real life in him.

A Note to Me

Dear Me,

I've known you for as long as I can remember.

I once heard there's "a friend who sticks closer than a brother," and yes, that's us, though I doubt it's what the proverb was talking about. I've been close to a lot of people, but you and me? We have quite an attachment.

Looking back, it's fair to say I've treated you pretty well. As a matter of fact, more times than I can count, I've put you ahead of anything and everything else. Agreed?

As we were growing up, I tried to make sure you were always at the front of the line. I saw to it that you got the biggest cookie on the plate, the best parking spot, the comfiest chair in any room we entered.

In school, I noticed the little things you liked, and I went after them. You always loved attention, so I did everything in my power to see that you got it. You still like the spotlight, so I've maneuvered to keep you in its glare. Now that we have the Internet, I have more tools. I post only the pictures that show you at your very best. Anybody would think you're living the dream. Have you seen the comments people write about you? When you have struggled or had a hard time, I've done my best to keep that our little secret. I've tried to make you happy.

Sure, it was a little easier to keep you happy when you were a cute little tyke. A simple temper tantrum got the job done. Then, as we grew older, I had to be a little more discreet. You wanted to keep winning and getting your way—all the while looking humble and unassuming. That gets tricky! Not to mention tiring.

Take marriage, for example. I promised to love and honor my wife, putting her needs ahead of my own, but you constantly insist on being first. Sometimes there's a little voice in my head in the middle of the night, saying, "*Pssst*, get up and take care of the baby, dude. Let the lady sleep." I know it's not *your* voice; you hate struggling out of bed at 3:00 a.m. You speak up and say, "Pretend you're still asleep," and, more often than not, I comply and put you before her.

Me, I know how you can get defensive, but you have had a tendency not to give me all the information. Walking through the sporting-goods store? Not your finest hour. I love to see you excited, but we should have taken a look at the budget first.

As a matter of fact, you never seem to care about dull stuff like bills and consequences and what happens tomorrow. I've said more than a few harsh words on your behalf to certain people, and you never warned me about the mess. You never told me I couldn't un-say what I've said.

I love you, Me. But I can't keep living for you. You always insisted that if I'd just keep you happy, then I'd be happy—as simple as that. But you know what? It's *not* as simple as that. It never has been.

Me, I've let you be in control and sit in the driver's seat, but it's clear you can't be trusted. You keep insisting you know the way we should go, but it always seems to be a dead end. I've looked into some other options, and I have decided to begin a journey down a different path. It's narrow and difficult and not many choose it, but it leads to real and abundant life. However—and there is no easy way to say this—I can't take this path if I bring you along.

So, Me, this is the end of you.

Sincerely,

Me

Part 1

Where Blessings Begin

Chapter 1

Broken to Be Whole

It's the middle of the night and I can't fall asleep.

Next thing I know, I'm in front of a computer screen. On that screen is YouTube. And on YouTube is a video called "Evolution of Dance."[1]

What, you've heard of it?

Sure you have. YouTube tells me this video has been viewed 286,488,088 times, and I know you're in there somewhere. Wait—

Okay, make it 286,488,089. I can't *not* watch it. But moving right along …

While I was fishing for another inspirational video, I experienced YouTube whiplash.[†] One minute Dude is twisting the night away, and the next I'm somehow watching a documentary about a poor community in Paraguay.

Yeah, quite a transition. At first, this new video is about what you'd expect to see—images of abject poverty. The community is literally located in a landfill, where more than 1,500 tons of trash are

---

† YouTube whiplash: a phenomenon that occurs when you inadvertently find yourself switching violently from one video genre to another.

dumped every day. Broken and discarded junk piled up everywhere, and that's home for these people.

More than one hundred residents scratch out a living by digging through the trash, looking for something that can be recycled and sold. I've seen it myself, firsthand, when I've visited developing-world countries. What YouTube can't give you is the *smell*. It's there in all these dumps: the smell of hopelessness.

It all seems broken beyond repair. But keep watching.

I soon learn that this community in Paraguay is known for something other than a landfill. Something you'd never guess, unless you've seen the video. This community is known for having—are you ready for this?—an amazing orchestra.

No, not your average, big-city philharmonic with Stradivarius violins and grand pianos played by the cast of the Grey Poupon commercial. No, it's a children's orchestra in which all the players live in the slums, right there at the landfill.

Favio Chavez, a young professional musician, happened to come for a visit. He was horrified by the living conditions he saw and that no one did anything about it. So he announced he was opening a small music school.

Before long he was surrounded by eager and willing candidates. They were ready to learn, but they had no instruments. However, Chavez had some ideas about that too. He'd met a trash picker, Nicolas Gomez, who could find almost anything in a mound of garbage. "I want you to look for a special kind of trash," Chavez told him. "Bring me anything we could recycle into an instrument."

But how?

Well, they made a cello from an oil can and old cooking tools, a flute from tiny cans, a drum set with old X-rays as the skins, a violin from a beat-up aluminum salad bowl and strings tuned with forks.

You or I, if we had visited, would have just seen and smelled and felt the sadness. Chavez *heard*—and he heard not what was, but what *could* be. He heard music emerging from squalor. The music of hope.

It's now known as the Landfill Harmonic, just to show that you can be in the dumps and still have a sense of humor. Here's an orchestra made of kids from a junkyard playing instruments built of refuse.[2] You can fire up the computer and watch it right now if you'll promise to stay away from that YouTube video about the talking cats.

You and I, we live in a throwaway culture. We'd never have thought of bringing beauty from recycling—not when Amazon.com, with shiny, brand-spanking-new stuff, is a click away. You break it? You trash it. You replace it.

Yet I go back to read the Gospels, and now there's a sound track. The music of the Landfill Harmonic seems to play on every page. I can hear it because I know the full story, and I see the connections. Jesus left the throne room of heaven for the landfill slum of earth. He gave up perfection for brokenness and pain. And he said, "Strike up the band." He heard weeping and wailing and turned it into laughter.

They called him a fool, a misguided fanatic. There was hopelessness all around him, but even if I gave you one hundred guesses, you'd never be able to come up with the full picture of what Jesus can do when he digs into that ugly hill and comes up with throw-away, busted fragments of life.

Sermon on the Mountainside

Jesus's best-known lesson is called the Sermon on the Mount—the mount being the location where he begins to teach his disciples about a new way of life.

He is in the midst of bringing God's kingdom to earth's landfill, and such things make people uncomfortable. Like the ideas of Chavez, this stuff runs counter to the ways people think. It says up is down and trash is treasure. He begins to introduce us to the great kingdom paradox: at the end of me, I find real life in him.

Matthew 5:1 tells us that Jesus sees the crowds, climbs a mountain, and sits down to teach. If you're like me, you tend to skip over that scene-setting stuff to get to the red-letter words in your Bible—the actual sayings of Jesus. But let's look a little deeper.

We find that if Jesus climbed a mountain, this is probably happening just above the Sea of Galilee. There were revolutionaries in those times, and a lot of them laid low in those mountains, avoiding arrest.

So this makes sense. Jesus is another revolutionary who has come up the mountainside. He is saying, "Down with the kingdom of this world and up with the kingdom of God." And the new kingdom has new rules, many of which are just the reverse of the old ways. Some New Testament scholars call this Jesus manifesto the "Great Reversal" for obvious reasons. Even today it all seems counterintuitive.

But Jesus doesn't want to talk about *tangible* rules or laws. He isn't into current events either. Nothing about the Romans here. All that is on the *surface* of life, and Jesus wants to go a little deeper to what's inside us—what makes the surface the way it is. The kingdom of God begins as an inside job.

Jesus launches his sermon with a list of very striking paradoxes. For our purposes we will look at four of these statements that sound ridiculous at first blush but start to make sense once you think a little deeper and compare your personal experience.

For example, his first statement promises the ultimate reward to the least likely people:

> Blessed are the poor in spirit, for theirs is the kingdom of heaven. (Matt. 5:3)

First four words: "Blessed are the poor." You might be thinking, *Yes! I win, because I'm completely broke.*

Then you stop to think about it. Maybe Jesus misspoke—surely it should be "Blessed are the rich." Because if you say to a rich person, "Hey, you have a beautiful mansion here," what does he say? "Yes, I know. I'm *so* rich." Nope. I bet he says, "Thank you. I'm so blessed."

And yes, I see the words *in spirit*, and I realize Jesus isn't talking about money for the most part. But the point remains. We think of a blessed life as one that ends up with plenty of money, not plenty of poverty. Add on the fact that Jesus uses a word for "poor" here that translates to "destitute" or "bankrupt."

Blessed are those who are bankrupt in spirit.

Really the word we use is *broke.*

Blessed are you when you're so broke you have nothing to offer.

If you think much about it, this is a shocking statement. Jesus is saying that God's kingdom begins in you when you come to the end of yourself and realize you have nothing to offer. It's precisely the opposite of every assumption we tend to make in this world.

Flat broke. Busted. How does that guy act? Not as if he's got the world on a string, all the answers neatly compiled. His spirits are in the gutter. And Jesus praises that here. That guy down in the dumps—he wins.

Yet the conventional wisdom of pretty much everywhere tells us to radiate self-confidence, self-sufficiency. In short, rich in spirit and in everything else to boot. Top of the heap, and not a garbage heap either.

Jesus says the kingdom begins with taking inventory and coming up with zero. We have nothing to offer, and that means we're making progress.

That's real revolutionary talk.

Sinful Simon

There's no review blurb from Jesus on the back of this book saying, *I'm okay; you're okay.* Jesus says nobody's okay. We're all broken. But what does that look like?

Luke 7 invites us to a dinner at the home of a religious leader named Simon, who is hosting the visiting rabbi, Jesus. Is Simon a Jesus enthusiast? Apparently not; his turn came up on the "host the rabbi" sign-up sheet, that's all. How do we know this? Luke makes it pretty clear.

You see, there was a protocol for this kind of evening. It was all spelled out in the rules. You'd greet the guest with a kiss of the hand, a sign of welcome. But Simon dispenses with this formality.

Also, foot washing was a daily reality in a dusty culture that revered cleanliness. The roads weren't exactly paved, so you washed your feet when you visited a friend. At this kind of dinner, the host was expected to help wash the visitor's feet.

Simon blew off this one too. At the very least, he could have offered a bowl of water and let Jesus have at it. But he didn't do that either.

Next on the checklist was anointing the guest's head with oil. This was an especially hospitable gesture, and very fine oil should be used, not the discount stuff from the drugstore. But, you guessed it, no anointment for Jesus.

Don't get me wrong. We don't stand much on ceremony at our place either. I don't have many books of dining etiquette on my shelf. I can't even keep my knives and forks straight when setting the table. My wife has it all down, but when she shows me for the 373rd time, I look at her lovingly and say, "Whatever."

Simon isn't saying that. He isn't trying and getting it wrong. He isn't trying at all, and he knows it; everybody in the room knows it. Remember, Simon is a religious leader, and right out in front of all the dignitaries, he's ignoring the religious rules. Which gives us a clue as to his opinion of the teachings of Jesus.

Simon is showing us how things tend to work. Because of his wealth, he is comfortable. Because of his power, he is respected, or at least feared. Because he's at the top of the heap, he's arrogant. This is a scenario everyone recognizes.

During the meal, a woman crashes the party. She has no invitation—she just walks in. Suddenly things are uncomfortable in a whole new way. Luke 7:37 identifies this woman as someone who "lived a sinful life." That's a polite way of saying she's a prostitute—and yes, she's checking in at a religious leader's home.

Simon surely is thinking, *What's up with this?* At the top of the heap, propriety is an important value. Nothing, in his mind, is more important than predictability and order. He's a professional religious rule follower.

So why does a prostitute show up at a dinner for the pious?

She must be feeling some blend of shame, humiliation, doubt—your choice of negative emotions.

But something brought her here. Has she heard about Jesus? Stood on the periphery of the crowd, listening to words about a kingdom too good to be true? Is she the very type of person who could use a Great Reversal?

Beautifully Broken

With daggers being stared at her from every direction, all this woman sees is Jesus. Or maybe we should put it this way: all she sees is Jesus seeing *her*.

As their eyes lock, there is no judgment, no looking at her as a mound of garbage that needs removal. She is broken and she knows it, but he sees something else.

She is *beautifully* broken.

Picture the scene. Jesus is reclining at the table. For some reason, chairs were not the thing. People hunkered down on the floor and leaned on an elbow that was propped up by a cushion. Their feet would reach away from the table.

As the woman approaches Jesus, she comes first to his feet—feet left filthy by Simon. At that moment, the room is silent. What could possibly happen next in this scenario between teacher and tramp?

She looks around hesitantly, knowing how most of the eyes will read: disgust, rejection, even outrage. Actually, many of them look down, awkward as people are in these situations. Or maybe some of these men fear she could call them by name, from past transactions.

Then she meets the gaze of Jesus, full and bold. He smiles; I'm sure of that. Her visit is treated as a delightful surprise. Treasure, not trash. He doesn't simply accept her—she seems to have made his day.

Because of this, she is undone.

She has come to the end of herself.

Tears begin to flow from her eyes, first just one or two and then a cascade. At this point all she can do is be real, because the love of Jesus is real. She falls to the floor and begins kissing his feet—dirt and sweat and all. The tears become the cleansing water Simon should have supplied.

The funny thing about tears is that when they fill our eyes, that's when we see most clearly. She knows that Jesus's feet haven't been washed. It's crystal clear what she must now do. But she can't exactly call to the host for a towel, can she? So she lets down her hair. In those days women always wore their hair up in public. If a woman let down her hair for a man who wasn't her husband, it was considered grounds for divorce—an act of indecency. So we can imagine the audible gasp that fills the room as she reaches to unfasten her hair.

Simon could have—should have—provided water from the well and the finest towel available. This woman, whose name we don't even know, provides water from her eyes and a towel from her hair. A dirty woman has become a living embodiment of cleansing.

That may sound nice, but it wouldn't have looked it. Not in those times. People in that room would be thinking, *I can't un-see this. It's a disgrace, a scandal!*

Then she brings out the perfume.

Women of the time often wore a small flask around their necks, filled with a bit of fragrance. For a prostitute, it would be an important part of daily business, a drop at a time, a man at a time.

Where one drop would have sufficed for the feet of a rabbi, she empties the flask. She will not need this ointment anymore. She offers all that she has because he has changed all that she is. She cannot stop kissing those feet, now clean in a way that turns the ritual inside out.

Just as his teaching does with every ordinary action. Just as he does now in addressing a supposedly righteous man and a supposedly wicked woman. His words turn every preconception inside out.

For Simon, Jesus has a rebuke.

For the woman, he has a blessing—and a word of redemption: "Your sins are forgiven" (Luke 7:48).

With those words, Jesus has enacted the beatitude "Blessed are the poor in spirit." He has blessed the poorest spirit imaginable and rebuked the gaudiest, richest, most arrogant.

Trick Question

Which person in the story do you want to be most like?

In the past when I've taught this story, I've asked the question, "Who are you most like?" but I think the real question we should struggle with is not who *are* you most like, but who do you *want* to be most like?

If you had to choose, would you be more like the well-respected religious leader who seems to have his stuff together, the guy everyone looks up to? The guy who lives in a beautiful home and has VIPs over for dinner?

Or would you rather be the broken prostitute who embarrasses herself but deeply experiences the love and grace of Jesus? The reason it's a trick question is because most of us want both, especially those of us who've been Christians for a while. Said another way, *we want to be made whole without having to be broken.*

We'd like to be Simon at the end of the story, saying, "Oh, okay—I get it. Good lesson, Jesus! I'll go on about my life, enjoying my wealth and status in a wiser way now."

Here's the only problem with that strategy: *we are all broken.*

It's true. Some of us just do a better job of hiding it than others. In Luke 7, it's painfully obvious that the woman is broken—she's lying on the floor, weeping, at a party she has crashed.

But what about Simon? This is a guy who has spent the first twelve years of his life memorizing the first twelve books of the Bible. By fifteen, he has memorized the entire Old Testament. Let that sink in for a moment. It means he can recite nearly three hundred prophecies about the coming Messiah. And at the moment he's looking across the table at him.

Yet Simon treats the Messiah as an unwanted dinner guest. Simon is broken too. He is *really* broken, which is defined as not knowing you're broken. The broken woman in the story knows goodness and perfection when she sees it; the broken man doesn't, and he doesn't even know that he doesn't.

Here's one to think about: the less you see your own brokenness, the more broken you are. Another one for the upside-down and inside-out file.

Don't misunderstand this chapter. I'm not here to break you. I'm not even asking you to break yourself. *You are already broken.* The Bible tells us in no uncertain terms, "All have sinned and fall short of the glory of God" (Rom. 3:23). The real question is whether we can own up to it.

It's not a question of being broken; it's a question of brokenness.

We Are "Those People"

Sociologist Brené Brown's TED talk on vulnerability has accumulated more than fifteen million hits. A significant factor in its popularity is the plain truth that, as much as we fight it, we long for the freedom to admit we're broken. We don't realize our need to do it. It's true for every one of us, and it's most true for those who least realize it.

Brown helps us see we're not alone. Here's what she says:

> We are "those people." The truth is … we are the
> others. Most of us are one paycheck, one divorce,
> one drug-addicted kid, one mental health diagnosis,

one serious illness, one sexual assault, one drinking binge, one night of unprotected sex, or one affair away from being "those people"—the ones we don't trust, the ones we pity, the ones we don't let our children play with, the ones bad things happen to, the ones we don't want living next door.[3]

We are *those people*.

We are the people who ignore the hurts of others, as long as someone takes care of us.

We are the people who yell at one another in the car on the way to church, then climb out with sunny smiles to demonstrate it's all good.

We are the people who think God is somehow more impressed with us because we make up our own rules and follow them.

We are the people who have gone into deep debt to keep up appearances.

We are the people who look down on others who are different.

We are the people who take the easy way out and log on to the porn site.

We are the people who work fifty-plus hours a week, trying to prove our worth.

We are the people with holes punched in our walls and doors unhinged from slamming.

We are the people who spend hours a day on social media, trying to convince people that our lives are better than theirs.

Most of us have some conception, in our heart of hearts, that a lot of the pieces never seem to be mended. But we will go to great lengths to avoid the full, honest embrace of our condition. There are just too many voices in our ears telling us not to sweat the small stuff, and it's all small stuff. Ask any of your Facebook friends, and they'll have you convinced in just a few quick words that you're not broken at all. Several hundred social media friends can't be wrong, can they?

There are too many voices telling us to keep up appearances, because if we don't, our life will fall apart.

There are too many voices telling us to entertain ourselves, and if we don't think the bad thoughts, the bad stuff will somehow trickle away.

That's why the people of our times have become masters of illusion, experts at covering pain, abusers of medication, slaves of financial debt, followers of fads, and partakers of loneliness. Because we won't realize that the only solution for being broken is … brokenness.

By brokenness, I mean the acknowledgment of it, the full and unflinching acceptance that we are bankrupt, poor in spirit, and have nothing to offer. In our culture, that's a hard sell. Few people will pay hundreds of dollars to attend a seminar helping them experience brokenness. They may not do it even if you pay them the hundreds of dollars.

Brokenness is not trending on Twitter. It's not written on anyone's résumé, and it's no business strategy at all. It is, however, the one hope Jesus holds out for us, the inside-out, upside-down way that is somehow the only path that ultimately is right side up.

Embrace the paradox: brokenness is the way to wholeness.

Real Life Begins

So the bad news is that I'm not okay and neither are you. We're both badly broken. Not "gently used," like the clothing requested by Goodwill. We're ripped, torn, and ragged. Citizens of the global junk heap.

The good news is that God makes the broken whole. He takes the overlooked, the undervalued, the left out, the written off, the damaged and destroyed, and then he does what only he can do.

God loves to make the broken beautiful.

In his book *Lord, Break Me,* William MacDonald points out that in the physical world, broken things lose their value. They are thrown away—glassware, dishes, furniture. Flaws are fatal. But in the spiritual world, just the reverse is true. Broken things are precious. Broken people reveal the beauty and power of God. Flaws are *openings*.

Jeremiah the prophet was sent by the Lord to a potter's house to await further instructions. When he got there, he saw the potter toiling away at his wheel, the water and clay mixing and whirling as a jar emerged. But the potter's fingers failed him at some delicate point, and he found himself holding a flawed jar, something no one would buy. As the prophet watched, the man pushed the clay back together and began molding it again, "as seemed best to him" (Jer. 18:4).

Then Jeremiah received further instructions from the Lord. "Can I not do with you, Israel, as this potter does?... Like clay in the hand of the potter, so are you in my hand, Israel" (v. 6).

It's such a beautiful image of God sitting at the wheel, looking down at a flawed piece of pottery, and refusing to toss it. The potter made another jar "as seemed best to him." All the same clay and the same cracks, but all made new. There *is* no junk heap. The art is in endless possibilities of one piece of clay.

My prayer is, *God, take my broken pieces and remold them into what seems best to you.*

The question is whether or not we are willing to let the cracks show. For some of us, nothing could be more unthinkable. We want to airbrush any mistakes or flaws or scars.

But God looks at our brokenness much more like something called Kintsugi. This is a ceramic restoration process developed in Japan in the fifteen hundreds. Broken ceramic pieces are sealed together, but instead of hiding the cracks, the cracks are boldly highlighted and traced over with gold.

Normally anything that was broken and refurbished sells at a discount, but not Kintsugi pottery. Most often, the ceramic piece actually turns out to be more beautiful and more valuable than before it was broken. In fact, many collectors have been accused of deliberately breaking prized ceramics so they could be made whole with gold. That sounds a lot like the economy in the kingdom of heaven. The broken are the most valuable.

This is the redeeming power of God through Jesus Christ. When we finally come to the end of ourselves and give God the broken pieces, he can make us whole. Isaiah 53:5 helps us see our brokenness from the perspective of the cross:

> But he was wounded for the wrong we did; he was
> crushed for the evil we did. The punishment, which
> made us well, was given to him, and we are healed
> because of his wounds. (NCV)

The word *wounded* in this verse actually refers to bruises—black-and-blue marks created by broken blood vessels. And the word *healed* comes from a root meaning "mended, repaired, thoroughly made whole." Isaiah is saying that we are made whole because he was broken.

And it's only after we have been made whole that we are ready to fulfill our purpose and be used by God. That's the inside-out way of Jesus—in you, then through you.

Cue the orchestra.

Chapter 2

Mourn to Be Happy

Toward the top of my list of least favorite things is waking up in the middle of an awesome dream.†

Don't you hate that? There you are, having this incredible dream with no connection at all to real life. Just good stuff for its own sake. Right at the best part, you wake up. Wait! No! You were in the middle of something!

It's especially annoying when the dream is clearly about escaping a load of stress. The dream is so good that what wakes you up is you telling yourself in the dream not to wake up.

When I was getting myself ready to write this chapter, I slept with a pen and paper beside my bed. The idea was that if I woke up from an awesome dream with no connection to real life, I could quickly write it down and remember it. I thought that was a killer

---

† Other least favorite things: unimportant emails marked urgent with a little red flag; grown men wearing socks with Crocs; how the barista at Starbucks looks confused when you say "large" instead of "venti"; people who don't turn right at a red light; Sudoku; people who make lists of things they don't like; irony.

idea, but the best I got was a dream of eating a bowl of sugary cereal.

Really? You know you're getting old and pathetic when your best dream is eating a bowl of Frosted Flakes instead of Fiber One.

But it seems a law of life that if you're in the middle of an awesome dream, something will wake you up.

Dream Intruders

They say life is but a dream, but if so, there are too many abrupt wake-ups in it. I bet you've had more than a few. I mean those times when life was on cruise control, but then something happened and you were suddenly in for a rough ride. The end of me often comes when my dreams come to an end.

Maybe for you it was pretty early on, when your mom or dad sat you down and introduced you to the word *divorce*.

Maybe it was a message from the person you thought was "the one," telling you it just wasn't going to work out.

Perhaps it was a phone call telling you there had been an accident and you needed to come to the hospital.

Maybe it was a text you were never supposed to read that uncovered the affair.

Maybe your boss told you the position you'd held for a number of years was being eliminated.

You were living the dream, and then life was shaking you awake. So intrusive. To come awake is to lose something—money, health, work, innocence, some special someone.

If you're going to live, you're going to lose. You will come to the end of yourself. You might as well wake up to the fact.

Six-Word Sagas

Ernest Hemingway made a bet. I imagine he made a number of them, but this one was with a group of authors over lunch, and it has since become an anecdote.

The guys bet him ten dollars he couldn't come up with a short story only six words long. Hemingway took that bet, pulled out a napkin, and wrote the following story on it:

For sale, baby shoes, never worn.

Hemingway understood the power of words, even just a few words, which was actually the essence of his style. They should have made the bet with one of the great Russian novelists, actually. There's certainly a story, and one that touches you, in those six words.

But you could do it too. You could give me six words—six different words—telling your story. What would they be?

- There has been a terrible accident.
- I'm leaving. The marriage is over.
- Your position is no longer needed.
- I just want to be friends.
- The cancer isn't responding to treatment.
- You are not able to conceive.
- Here's a rose off the casket.

You've gone from dreaming to mourning. But if things were different? What if you could reverse the equation, wake up from a nightmare to a dream? What if your mourning could lead to a blessing?

Jesus turns another one inside out and upside down. In the midst of loss and deep disappointment, when it feels like we are coming to the end of ourselves, he turns the page and shows us a new story of hope and redemption.

As he continues that sermon, preached on the mountain near the Sea of Galilee, Jesus shows us another way life looks different through his kingdom lens. He suggests that in God's kingdom, the item with the hefty price tag is now marked way down, and the cheap giveaway is now extremely valuable. The billionaire is henceforth a bum. The homeless guy is king.

Let's look at a little more context for this sermon in Matthew 5–7. Matthew lets us know that a huge crowd is there to hear Jesus preach. The word for *crowd* really means "a large group of unidentified people." Over my years as a public speaker, I've learned something about large groups of unidentified people: they are tightly packed with stories of heartache and shattered dreams. To gather people is to gather sad stories, and this would be true even at a convention of department-store Santas.

I am especially aware of this when I stand to preach at my home church. Though not purposefully, my eyes fall on the people I know—people who've had life wake them up from their dreams. Over to the left are the parents whose daughter is battling cancer; toward the back is the widow who dreads going home to a lonely house after church. And on the right, the young man who just left rehab for the third time.

Sometimes I see a couple separated by half the auditorium. And I know the story of that space too. I know a few stories here and there, but Jesus knows them all.

I wonder if Jesus scanned his crowd up on the mountain and saw countless sad narratives, shoulder to shoulder. We don't know what he was thinking, but we're taken aback by what he was *saying*—and the crowd must have been too. He opens with the Beatitudes, a list of reverses that changes the retail price of everything. Blessings: everything you know about them is wrong.

We've considered the first beatitude: "Blessed are the poor." Yeah, right! Good one, Jesus! Who feels more blessed in life than folks with plenty of nothing? Eyes would roll. This rabbi has got to be kidding. And then he throws out the next one and ups the ante.

Blessed are …

What will it be? Based on how this world works, in your experience, how would you complete his sentence? Blessed are:

- Those whose wildest dreams come true.
- Those who get the best jobs.
- Those who marry supermodels.

Here's how Jesus finishes it:

Blessed are those who mourn, for they will be comforted. (Matt. 5:4)

Wait. What? "Those who mourn"? That's all he's got?

Sitting down on a first-century mountain, in an age of infant mortality, of short life spans, of hunger, of disease, of national humiliation, he says those words.

"Those who mourn" make up a significant fraction of that audience. And none of them step forward to testify, to say, "Yes sir! Mourning rules!"

We've said that Jesus was speaking in paradoxes, but aren't we past paradox territory now? We've gone over the county line into Ludicrous-ville. Contradiction-land. Jesus is saying something like, "Happy are the sad."

Mourning Our Circumstances

A nice start would be figuring out what Jesus is thinking about when he uses the word *mourning*. The Bible offers a few examples.

First, we mourn the true circumstances of life.

These are the dream-busters that awaken us at the worst time. We don't choose them. We don't invite them. They just kick down the door and come in. Something beyond our control that changes everything.

I'd love to give you five handy tips for keeping the dream-busters out, but the truth is, it can't be done. Life has a way of waking everybody up at some point. Everybody has that sudden, painful longing for yesterday, when they didn't know how good they had it, just before the world fell in.

When that happens—and if it hasn't, it will—Jesus says, *You are blessed.*

Maybe you can squint at it just right, take it as poetry, and have it sound appealing. Nice words you might embroider with swirly flowers and give to a lonely widow in the nursing home. Or you could take it as a Zen-type thing, like "the sound of one hand clapping"—something heavy that's supposed to sound cool but actually doesn't make any sense.

But the poetry falls apart once you fill in the for-instances. Try a couple of these:

- It's a blessing to be a young widow raising four small children.
- It's a blessing to lose your job and count down the days to losing your house.
- It's a blessing to be a recovering alcoholic with almost nothing left.
- It's a blessing to lose your husband to a woman he met on a business trip.
- It's a blessing to watch a parent doing a slow fade into the fog of Alzheimer's.

This next one is for you to personalize:

It's a blessing to _____.

So, what's it all about, Jesus? What does that little phrase even mean?

Maybe he's excluding the worst stuff. Maybe this is limited to a bad day at the office, a minor fender bender, a mild dustup in the committee meeting.

We don't mind the little "character builder" moments, like setting the alarm clock to p.m. instead of a.m. by accident and getting to work late. Or placing your phone in the cup holder of the car without looking, only to find there's a cup, of all things, with several inches of Diet Coke still in it. Or not being able to think of a third random example to add to this paragraph.

At that level we can say, "That was annoying, but we'll laugh about it later. And realize we are so blessed!"

But when a teenager is in the intensive care unit after a serious collision, you don't sit in the waiting room and say, "We'll laugh about this later." And the problem is, the evidence tells us this is the one Jesus is talking about. He didn't spend a lot of time on petty annoyances, actually. He's speaking about the end-of-me moments in life.

He uses the word *mourn*, and that means what happens inside us when we experience significant, major-league suffering.

The commentator William Barclay did a good job giving us the weight of the word. He wrote, "The Greek word for *to mourn*, used here, is the strongest word for mourning in the Greek language.… It is defined as the kind of grief which takes such a hold that it cannot be hidden. It is not only the sorrow which brings an ache to the heart; it is the sorrow which brings the unrestrainable tears to the eyes."[1]

Sure. But where is the blessing in that?

If the Beatitudes were describing how we view blessing from a cultural perspective, we would read something like, "Blessed are you when everything goes your way." Or, "Blessed are you when all your dreams come true." A blessed life, as any normal person would define it, would be a life free from mourning, not a life marked by it!

We can't spin this one, parse this one, or twist this one around without Jesus twisting it right back. He says that when we mourn—when life gets extremely difficult, when we experience the deepest suffering we've ever encountered, when we come to the end of ourselves—then we are blessed.

It seems upside down. But maybe the problem is that we've spent so much of our lives looking at something upside down that it seems right side up to us. As wild as it sounds, consider the possibility that the whole world is crazy and Jesus has it right.

If so, then his message would be that blessing isn't dependent on what happens on the outside. It comes from the inside—and there is a blessing to be found only through the shedding of a certain number of tears.

I've asked you to consider the possibility that Jesus is right, but I know he is because I've been there and experienced what he's talking about. It's the blessing that can be found only at the end of your dreams, when you come to the end of yourself.

Blessed by His Presence

It works like this. In surprising ways, suffering makes room in our spirit for us to know and experience the blessing of God's peace and presence. Without suffering, we simply can't know his comfort. In mourning, we experience the blessing of God's presence.

In the Old Testament book of Job, Satan was looking forward to Job's suffering. Job was experiencing what most of us would call a blessed life. He was rich, happily married, living the good life. But storms—really nasty storms—were on the horizon, and Satan figured it would all go down a certain way. He thought, sad to say, like many of us think, that once the bad stuff came, Job would hold it against God and declare his religion invalid and useless.

The first chapter of the book tells us that Job had seven sons, three daughters, seven thousand sheep, three thousand camels, five hundred yoke of oxen, and five hundred donkeys, not to mention a small army of servants. So that was the starting point.

Then Job became a kind of case study of faith in suffering because he lost nearly everything, bit by bit. A strong wind knocked down his house and killed his children. But the book of Job was just getting started. In the second chapter, Job lost his health. He was infested with sores over every inch of his body. He lost all his livestock and all his wealth, and Satan was betting on him losing all his faith in the bargain. His wife's best advice was, "Curse God and die!" (2:9). Because what good is God if life doesn't work out for a time?

To Satan's befuddlement, Job experienced God in a way he never had before. "My ears had heard of you," he said, "but now my eyes have seen you" (42:5).

Here's what we find in our suffering. There is a deep void that used to be filled with whatever we lost. That could be stuff or even relationships—none of which are bad things. But when it's gone, it leaves an aching cavity, and God is there to fill it up with himself.

When we suffer, we mourn.

When we mourn, we are comforted by "the God of all comfort" (2 Cor. 1:3).

Blessed are those who mourn.

Everyone experiences loss, and no one is overjoyed by it. Black is black. Except when it isn't. Let's write another six-word story. You'll especially understand this one if you're reading it through tear-filled eyes:

God will not waste your pain.

Here's another one:

God will not leave you alone.

Eugene Peterson's *The Message* paraphrases Matthew 5:4 this way: "You're blessed when you feel you've lost what is most dear to you. Only then can you be embraced by the One most dear to you."

At the end of yourself, you have an opportunity to experience the presence of God in a way you never have before. Maybe you've embraced some wonderful things and lost them. But there's no embrace like the divine one.

Embrace the Pain

We do everything we can to stay away from suffering in the first place. But when we do suffer, which is inevitable, we do everything we can to stay away from mourning. Then, when we catch ourselves mourning, we do all in our power to make it go away.

We numb ourselves with entertainment. We medicate the pain with drinking, shopping, working, or partying. It's a grim quest to turn that frown upside down, but we are convinced that's what it means to be blessed.

Then we find the frown won't stay away. Gravity just keeps tugging at the edges. We're going to suffer—but they can't make us mourn! We shift our efforts to getting over it. Getting past it. Getting around it. We "get over" the broken heart of a wrecked relationship, the debilitating regret of a disastrous decision, or the impossible options of a serious illness by living in denial, blaming others, or basking in guilt.

Recently *Good Morning America* told about a man named Jeff Goldblatt. He will be remembered as the founder of Get Over It Day. Since I know you'll want to mark your calendar, it happens on March 9.[†] You can even google the Get Over It Day website, which is jam-packed with helpful hints for just saying no to grief. Come March 10, maybe you'll have plowed right past all your suffering. Just a matter of hitting the emotional accelerator.

Or not.

I get it though. It's human nature to avoid suffering. Asking for a second helping of sadness seems more than a little unnatural. Jesus isn't recommending that you take up suffering as a weekend hobby. He just wants you to realize that you can find an incredible blessing hidden in the shadows. And that blessing might be visible only through the lens of your tears.

Dick and Elizabeth Peterson were happily married and enjoying life. Then one day she was diagnosed with multiple sclerosis. Dick

---

†   If you are reading this on March 9, it may be a sign that it really is time for you to get over it. Also, national Check Your Batteries Day often falls on March 9. When your smoke alarm wakes you up in the middle of the night, maybe you'll appreciate these footnotes a little more. You're welcome.

knew the going would be tough. What he didn't realize was that he would come to know more of Jesus than he ever thought possible.

As the "intruder" invaded his wife's body, it was as if it invaded his as well. He watched her move from a cane to a walker and on to a wheelchair, and every setback was his setback—*their* setback. His life was dramatically affected by her increasing needs. Together they realized they were utterly out of control, as their lives spiraled more and more into devastation. There was only one path, the one set by the disease, and it grew narrower and narrower.

They prayed for healing with every ounce of faith they had. Their family prayed. Their church prayed. They heard of miracles and wondered if God might have one for them. And if he didn't, why not?

The questions themselves were a form of suffering, but there was something else they had to admit—a possibility they had never considered. Maybe something wasn't just being done *to* them—but *for* them.

What a shocking, outlandish, unexpected thought.

One day Elizabeth asked her husband, "Did it really take this to teach me that my soul is more important to God than my body?"

Dick asked God, "Was this the cost of teaching me compassion?"

They had thoughts, insights, and aha moments they'd never anticipated, all of them concerning the ways of God. As they prayed for Elizabeth to get her old life back, it occurred to them that God cared a lot more about her experiencing a *new* life. A deeper one. A wiser one.

They prayed for change on the outside. God cared more about change on the inside. They prayed for their desires and realized more and more that God answered in terms of their needs.

As Dick shares, the intruder, the ugly disease, is still in their home—still unwelcome, still making new demands every day. And still teaching precious lessons, unavailable any other way, about submission, dependence, service, and the kind of love Paul describes in 1 Corinthians 13. There's nothing life can throw at us that God can't use to draw us nearer to him.

The tears bring their own focus, and they begin to make the intruder look strangely like a guest.

When disaster comes, we can't see anything bigger than what we've lost. But the truth is, God more than fills that space. We begin to see that he's not just filling *that* space, but spaces we didn't even know we had.

Everyone experiences loss. Everyone mourns. But those who follow Jesus find that their pain is not wasted. There is a blessing that seems totally illogical. It requires climbing to the bottom of the deepest pit, without a flashlight, venturing far into the darkness.

But the blessing is there, and it's worth everything.

Mourning Our Sin

So far we've approached mourning as our response to the tragic circumstances of life. That's the most common understanding of the word. But the Bible speaks about another form of the process.

There is also the mourning that is our response to the sin in ourselves and in our world. The first kind of mourning is inspired by devastation from without. This one springs from devastation from within—the sinfulness that wreaks havoc on us, on those we love, and on the world around us. Throughout Scripture there's a connection between mourning over sin—of every kind—and receiving God's blessing. Israel often mourned together as a nation and received God's blessing as a nation.

There's an intriguing example of this kind of mourning in the Old Testament. David, you may remember, had an affair with Bathsheba. In time, the magnitude of his sin came crashing down on him, and he was utterly distressed, distraught, undone. He mourned from the depths of his soul. And David had a very deep soul.

In Psalm 32, he talks about the period of time before he took on that mourning. On the surface he actually would have appeared happier. Denial puts on a positive face. But at the soul level, it was a different story. He was missing out on a life-changing, faith-altering blessing from God:

> Blessed is the one whose transgressions are forgiven,
> whose sins are covered. Blessed is the one whose
> sin the LORD does not count against them and in
> whose spirit is no deceit. (vv. 1–2)

The word *blessed* is used twice in these two sentences. But that's not the only word. *Sin* appears twice too.

An interesting word, *sin*. A century or so ago, our vocabulary was rich in synonyms for *sin*. Words like *iniquity. Transgression. Turpitude. Depravity. Reprobation.* And my personal favorite: *peccancy.* New Testament Greek had thirty-three different words for *sin*. Apparently we once knew our way around that concept.

You can learn a lot about a society by digging through their heap of discarded words. These days you don't hear people worrying about their turpitude at the water cooler or sharing about their depravity during prayer request time.

I read that a few years ago the *Oxford Junior Dictionary*, having long since scratched out the words listed above, tried to make it a clean sweep by removing the word *sin*. Supposedly it was an old, decrepit word that now sat in the corner of the vocabulary parlor, rocking in its chair and talking about the old days. Nobody paid attention to that one anymore. Cousin Iniquity and Cousin Turpitude, well, they passed away, and the children don't come to visit much. Children? *Mistake. Unfortunate Choice.* And of course, little *Boo-boo*.

To be honest, I feel this tension as a preacher. We tend to tweak the word *sin* and substitute *mistake* or one of those other more innocuous phrases. Sin is "preachy." It wags its finger at us too much. It meddles. So we talk about *unfortunate choices* or *slipups*.

But those words don't really fit, do they? If I step on your foot, that's probably a mistake. My bad, but I didn't mean to do it! I'm just clumsy.

On the other hand, if I don't like you and I intentionally stomp on your foot as hard as I can—that's no mistake. Now we're in sin territory.

Another word that pinch-hits for *sin* is *disease*. It brings a whole no-fault concept with it. I shouldn't have robbed that bank, but, you know—it's my *disease*. I'm wired that way. I have an *addiction* to entering banks with a gun and taking bags of money.

Can sin be addictive? Absolutely. Nothing is more addictive than sin, which seeks to enslave us. But once we buy into the notion that we're sinners with no control over our actions, we've missed something. Or we want someone else to.

We can wipe *sin* out of our dictionaries. If only we could wipe it out of our souls. As a culture, we can try to rub out the definition of *sin*, but the condition isn't going anywhere. It cracks the whip on just as many slaves—the entire population of the world—as it ever did. If we fail to acknowledge its reality, there can be no mourning. And without mourning there can be no confession. And without confession we miss the richest blessing of God's forgiveness and grace.

So don't call it a mistake, an addiction, a boo-boo, or "my bad." Call it sin.

Around 1,600 years ago, Augustine wrote in his *Confessions,* "My sin was all the more incurable because I did not think myself a sinner."[2] That's why preachers need that word that tells a vast story in only three letters. Without seeing the depths of sin, we'll never understand the heights of God's love and grace.

Jesus said when we're forgiven much, we love much (see Luke 7:47). Seeing myself in painful perspective allows me to rejoice in full fidelity. I know how great God's mercy is, because I know how little I deserve it. The deeper my mourning, the greater a party I need to throw, because something miraculous has happened.

In Psalm 32 David goes on to say,

> When I kept silent, my bones wasted away through
> my groaning all day long. For day and night your
> hand was heavy on me; my strength was sapped as
> in the heat of summer. Then I acknowledged my
> sin to you and did not cover up my iniquity. I said,
> "I will confess my transgressions to the LORD." And
> you forgave the guilt of my sin. (vv. 3–5)

Denial seems like a good idea at the time. It's the path of least resistance. But you don't want to go where that path leads. Sometimes the rugged road is the only one to the best destination.

Have you experienced the blessing of facing up to sin?

It's amazingly liberating. We put so much energy into running away, hiding, and pretending someone else did it. Or that the hole we dug wasn't really so deep. Or that we were somehow helping the person we hurt deeply.

Meanwhile, as we run, we feel our strength draining away as David did. No amount of time at the gym will make up for it—there's a leak somewhere, and it seems to be coming from deep inside.

Sooner or later we stop running, usually because we've run out of places to run to. We finally let the tears come, and that's when we find the missing strength. The twist is that it's not our strength at all. It's the power of God's arms wrapped around us. And at the end of me, I find the richest of blessings.

The Opposite of Mourning

As I studied this inside-out teaching, I asked myself, *What is the opposite of mourning or weeping?*

Well, surely the opposite of mourning is laughter. Now, how does our culture often react to the idea of sin around us? What do stand-up comedians and late-night TV hosts build their acts around? What do the sitcoms make light of?

Sin is a laughing matter today, a matter for mockery. If mourning is a path to take, then laughter moves precisely in the opposite direction on the spiritual compass. And as I've studied this material,

I've been struck—the word is *convicted*—by this insight. I like to laugh, like most people. But how often do I laugh at the very things that should cause me to mourn?

Remember, we originally defined this second form of mourning as our response to the sin in ourselves *and in the world around us.*

So is anyone out there mourning?

Where is the man who weeps over his selfishness and pride?

The woman who weeps over her gossip and her vanity?

The husband who weeps over his passivity and the years, long gone, when he could have led his family?

Where is the wife who weeps over her unsubmissive and critical spirit?

Where is the student who weeps over his cheating, his lust, his ingrained cynicism?

Where is the Christian who reads the news and sees the sin in our culture and feels the bruising in his inner spirit? There is a joy and peace that come only when we finally let ourselves see the sin and let our eyes shed tears for it. Because in the midst of all those tears, all that grief, is where God's blessing can be found. I realize it sounds a little crazy, but more and more I actually feel something like gratitude that I'm able to mourn my sin before God. There's pain in confession, and then, on the other side, there's a feeling like cool water washing over me on a blazing hot day.

So, let's be clear. You will fall into sin. Everyone does. And you'll still be slow to face your mourning. Everyone is. Just understand that in your hesitancy to mourn your sin, you're also delaying the blessing of God. There is no way to get to that blessing without the mourning that precedes it.

David, a pretty good poet, says, "Do not be like the horse or the mule, which have no understanding but must be controlled by bit and bridle or they will not come to you" (Ps. 32:9). Short version: *Don't be an idiot.* Where you need to go, where your heart really wants to go, go willingly.

Then there's verse 11. I love this one. David has told us about sin, about confession, about the wonderfulness of God's forgiveness and righteousness, and he punctuates the whole discussion like this: "Rejoice in the LORD and be glad, you righteous; sing, all you who are upright in heart!"

You've been through the dark night of the soul, the heaviness of the mourning, and now the sun is bright and the day is beautiful. It's time for the party—the prodigal has come home, the weary road behind him.

At the end of me is singing and rejoicing!

The Essential Penitential

Mourning isn't a "no big deal" thing. It isn't an "okay if you're into that" thing. It isn't a "think positively and it will go away" thing. It's a necessary thing. And it's a very good, very beneficial thing. A blessing thing.

What if you tried this? What if you faced the sin in your life this very day with a period of genuine mourning? What if you spent some time meditating, praying, and grieving over the sin in the world around you?

Before you think about all that, think about this: it's going to change you. It's going to transform your outlook on yourself and your world in a dramatic way. In essence, you're electing to see things from Christ's perspective, from the inside out, and you can't do that without becoming a little more like Christ.

Here's James's advice to you:

> Come near to God and he will come near to you. Wash your hands, you sinners, and purify your hearts, you double-minded. Grieve, mourn and wail. Change your laughter to mourning and your joy to gloom. Humble yourselves before the Lord, and he will lift you up." (4:8–10)

Since repentance and mourning don't come naturally to us, let me offer some questions to ask yourself to start you on this penitent path that leads to blessing.

- How have I sinned in the last few days?
- Who else has been hurt by my sin?
- Besides confessing to God, is there someone I need to apologize to?
- How can I clean up the mess my sin made?
- Whom will I confess my sins to?
- What excuses and justifications have I just come up with in answering these questions?

They had some really compelling traditions in the Old Testament, and we should take a closer look at a few of them. One is called *penitential mourning*. It was usually a period of seven to thirty days, and it was a time for the whole community to grieve together over its sin. People sometimes wore sackcloth as an outer expression of their inner mourning—to visually communicate that they were at the end of themselves.

You know where I'm going with this. I challenge you to join me for a time of penitential mourning. Seven days sounds about right. Instead of putting on a happy face, you'll let the tears come. You'll invite them.

I don't have any fashion advice on trendy sackcloth attire, but you might want to cut a strip of some coarse fabric and tie it around your wrist for the duration. It will remind you of what's at the top of your agenda for that week.

There is regret, and then there's regret for being caught. Mourning is true and focused grief, just you and God, and it's often marked by tears. Back in the sixteen hundreds, the Puritan Thomas Watson said it this way: "Tears melt God's heart and bind His hand."

It's a far cry from the "have a nice day" faith we tend to preach. I realize that. It's not too perky or peppy. But it happens to be aligned with truth, and it happens to be the one path to the deepest, fullest joy that God offers. You'll walk through the valley of the shadow, but I promise you this: you'll never walk alone.

The blessing awaits.

Chapter 3

Humbled to Be Exalted

Great news! The odds say you aren't going to die in an avalanche.

Seriously, I looked it up. Avalanches kill only about thirty people per year in the United States, which means you're looking really good for avoiding a demise of this nature.

Still, I'd be remiss if I didn't let you know you could still *be* in an avalanche. If it did actually happen to you, I wouldn't want your lack of preparation to be on my conscience.

In case it does happen, here's an important avalanche survival tip:[†] *Spit first. Dig second.*

That's it. Pretty simple, right?

Turns out one of the biggest mistakes people make when caught in an avalanche is that, once they're covered over with tons of snow, they dig blindly trying to get out. The *dig* part is a good idea. *Blindly*, not so much. It's too easy to dig in the wrong direction, burrowing deeper into the snow.

[†]   You're actually five times more likely to be killed by a falling coconut. But I couldn't find any helpful tips for surviving death by coconut.

Popular Science magazine wrote about one such victim. When rescue teams found his body, they discovered that in his furious attempts to dig out, he'd accidentally dug some thirty feet *deeper*. The victim expended every ounce of strength he had, only to get himself farther from his intended goal. If only he had spit first!

What, still not getting it?

Okay, if you're covered with snow, then there's almost no way to tell which direction is which, but gravity still applies. So push some snow away from your face … and spit. If the spit falls directly away from you, then you're facing down and you need to turn around. If the spit falls left or right, you're sideways. This is maybe the only time you ever want to spit in your own face. Because if you do, you're facing up, and in that situation, up is good.

When a man spits, he knows up from down. I'm sure somebody, somewhere, has said that at some point. Probably a crusty old mountain man. So when it's over, when you're safe at home in front of a warm fire, enjoying a mountain-man beverage, let that be a reminder to send me a thank-you note. Or a gift card. That's up to you.

When Jesus came on the scene as a rabbi, there was a lot of directional confusion. Up seemed like down. People were trying to find the light, but they only dug themselves deeper. It was a time of confusion, much like today. And it was what the Bible calls "the fullness of time," when Jesus came to set the compass once and for all.

When Jesus sets things in order, why does it sound as if he's holding the map upside down? Need more evidence? Consider the third beatitude. Jesus says the way down is up and the way up is down.

God blesses those who are humble, for they will
inherit the whole earth. (Matt. 5:5 NLT)

Again, we hear this through twenty-first-century ears and
it comes across as some kind of irony. The humble are inheriting
the earth? Really? Because it looks an awful lot like the CEOs, the
Hollywood stars, the reality TV stars, and the movers and shakers
have dibs. *Humble* isn't the word that comes to mind when you go
over that list.

Yet Jesus insists on this idea, even here in Luke:

For all those who exalt themselves will be humbled,
and those who humble themselves will be exalted.
(18:14)

It's a radical reversal, and it sounds great. The overlooked ones,
the quiet ones, and the ones you tend to forget are in the room have
their day, while the loud ones, the demanding ones, and the entitlement crowd are thrown under the bus. We'd love to put Humble
Guy Day on the calendar.

But when does this actually happen, Jesus? And how?

Directionally Challenged

Jesus says the way up is down. Greatness is humility.

In Luke 18, Jesus tells a parable to help us compare the two
directional systems—his and the world's. It's a story of two men.
One is a Pharisee. The Pharisees were a group of people reacting

against the increasing religious compromise of the Jewish people. Quite understandably, they wanted to bring back the old-time religion, which was being lost in the cultural upheaval of the time.

People looked up to Pharisees because these guys were sold out, committed to the Hebrew law, and tended to be upstanding, educated, and influential. We'd place them at the top of the social scale.

Down on the bottom we'd find the other guy in this story. He was a tax collector.

Remember the prostitute in chapter 1? Even she looked down on the tax man. To think of him as a first-century IRS agent doesn't really get the idea across. He was more like an IRS agent who belonged to terror cells. Not only did he collect taxes for the Romans, but he also was allowed to dip into people's wallets a second time to line his own pockets. He was basically a traitor and a legalized thief.

So two guys walk into the temple. One is the kind you point out to your son and say, "See this man? That's what you should be when you grow up." And the other is the kind you point out to your son and say, "Help me collect some rocks."

Who is Jesus's audience? Luke clues us in. They were people "who were confident of their own righteousness and looked down on everyone else" (v. 9). Wouldn't you agree that's a loaded description? The word *smug* comes to mind. So does *condescending*. This is a one-two jab to the upturned nose. Things would have gotten a little bit uncomfortable because everyone would know whom Jesus is talking about. For example, if I were preaching a sermon in Louisville, Kentucky, and referred to a group of rednecks who think they are better than everyone else, people would know whom I was talking about.[†]

When we read something like that, it's easy to think of others who fit that description.[‡] We almost immediately assume this description is about someone other than ourselves. But as soon as we assign these descriptors to other people, we ourselves become the very people Jesus is addressing.[§]

Everyone in the crowd recognized Jesus's characters. But did they see the target on their own clothing? When we hear a good zinger in church, we always tend to assume it's about somebody over in the next pew. We think, *I hope she takes this to heart,* rather than, *Does this fit me?* Which, when talking about pride and arrogance, confirms our own guilt.

Jesus is talking to a crowd of people who think he's talking to a whole other crowd of people. Which is so often the case.

So, as I was saying, two guys walk into the temple. Both of them have come to pray, which is pretty natural. The Pharisee, respected religious leader and all-around good guy, lifts up a prayer about himself:

> God, I thank you that I am not like other people—
> robbers, evildoers, adulterers—or even like this tax
> collector. I fast twice a week and give a tenth of all
> I get. (vv. 11–12)

---

†   Answer: Kentucky fans. (Not to worry, they don't read.)

‡   Tip: If reading this with a small group, avoid making eye contact with others in the room.

§   Oops. Sorry, Kentucky fans. My bad.

Apparently he's peeking during the middle part of the prayer. He spots a tax collector and uses him as a prop to stand on for extra righteousness—before adding on words of praise for his own giving and piety: "I fast twice a week, Lord, and I tithe every penny before taxes. But of course you knew that. I'm just saying. Amen."

Here's something else you need to know about the Pharisees. Because they lived in a time in which people were losing touch with their religious heritage, the Pharisees became obsessive about religious rules, since so many of those rules were being ignored. This made them a kind of roving "gotcha" patrol.

That's how the Pharisees, who began with all kinds of good intentions, pushed the faith of Israel into an unbearable, nearly infinite collection of dos and don'ts—mostly don'ts.

God had given those rules for the sake of people, but in a Pharisee's mind, people lived for the sake of rules.

You May Be a Pharisee If ...

Did you notice? The Pharisee's prayer started with a "thank you," just as many praise psalms do. Seems like a good start, right? You're thanking God for his blessings and goodness. This guy, however, identifies *himself* as the blessing. "Thank you, God, for the miracle of me." To heighten the effect, he rounds up the usual suspects from the local hall of villainy, comparing his righteousness to their wrongeousness.

Of course, we ourselves would *never* pray anything like that, right? Again I feel compelled to point out that once we've said that or thought that, we've just convicted ourselves. This thing is kind of a trap, isn't it?

That's a big issue with pride versus humility. Fake humility expresses itself in a pride that is obvious to everyone but the speaker. The Bible says, "The mouth speaks what the heart is full of" (Matt. 12:34). Ultimately our words betray us, no matter how much we guard them.

What are the verbal symptoms of a prideful heart? How can you tell if an internal Pharisee is about to flow out of your mouth?

You may be a Pharisee if ...

- **you catch yourself saying, "You aren't going to talk like that to me!"**

   Pride makes us defensive and unwilling to hear criticism or correction. What we're saying here is, "I'm immune from that kind of advice." It's also assuming a hierarchy in which we outrank the other person. We're taken aback that anyone would offer correction. We respond in an insulted, arrogant tone, and sometimes, if we're not too far gone, we think, *Where did that come from?*

   If there are no people in your life who offer you loving feedback and criticism, it's not because you've grown beyond it. I hope this isn't news to you. You might be thinking, *Nobody offers me advice, because they can't find anything to criticize.* I can assure you the truth is closer to this: nobody offers you advice because they know it's not going to end well if they do.

- **you catch yourself saying, "I'm not going to be the one to apologize."**

Proverbs tells us, "Pride only leads to arguments" (13:10 NCV). The proud are magnetically attracted to conflict. And when the proud get into a squabble, it can become epic, because the hardest thing in the world would be for them to apologize. That requires humility.

Some words and phrases just won't come out of the prideful mouth. "I was wrong. Please forgive me," for example. It's agonizing because it feels like defeat, and proud people are obsessive about being undefeated in arguments, class discussions, political conversations, and family disputes. And proud people love to make their point on the Internet.

The few, the proud (unfortunately the proud are not few) will wait out the worst disagreements without apologizing. They can hold out for decades, kind of hoping it all blows over. "I was wrong" or "that was my fault" are out of the question. On the very, very rare occasion one of the proud apologizes, he'll qualify it: "I'm sorry—but ..." Qualified apologies never seem to work.

- **you catch yourself saying, "It's not fair."**

The question here is, how do we define fair? If I feel I'm more deserving than everybody around me, a lot of things are going to seem unfair. Why did she get that raise? Why does he get to live in such a big house? Why did they make him an elder at church? Why is everybody always saying nice things about her?

Here's a clue: if you have a hard time celebrating with others in their successes or victories, you're probably suffering from a case of pride. And if you lack gratitude for the good things in your life, it's the same problem.

If you think you're all-deserving, why should you feel thankful for anything? You've got it coming to you. If you tend to feel entitled, if you're never quite content with the way credit is doled out, if you're overly concerned that everybody knows your accomplishments—you just might be a Pharisee.

- **you catch yourself whispering, "Did you hear about ..."**

Pharisees love the latest gossip. It tends to put other people in their proper place, and it underlines how superior they themselves are. We can always find a tax collector or two in the room. Other people and their antics are convenient steps for us to climb on our journey to the top of the human heap.

- **you catch yourself saying, "I don't need anybody's help."**

Notice how the Pharisee in the parable never asks for God's help? "Just checking in, God—it's all under control." He wants God to know he's got checkmarks in all the right boxes—his giving, his fasting. God really couldn't get along without him.

Pride keeps us from realizing how desperately we need God.

What are your prayers like? If they are filled with complaining and self-justification, then you just might have a pride issue, and this parable is for you.

• **you catch yourself saying, "It's not me; it's you."**

That sounds like the mirror image of one of the classic breakup lines, but in this case it's a function of the twenty-twenty vision Pharisees have in detecting the flaws of others. Yet they seem to cast no reflection in mirrors. The Bible points out that pride is blinding. You can't see the pride in your life because of ... well, because of the pride in your life.

Last week I was driving my kids to school. My nine-year-old son asked me a good one. "Dad," he said, "why do you always talk to the other drivers? You know they can't hear you."

But of course *he* could. And I thought about the things he could hear me saying. What he didn't hear was a dad speaking words of life and encouragement to the community of fellow travelers; a dad taking responsibility or apologizing for his own bad moves behind the wheel.

It's always the other guy … or gal, as is often the case.[†] See what I'm doing here? Besides digging myself a hole, I'm pointing out that it's someone else's problem, not mine, and not even my gender. We can see it in other people, and we know what they should do differently, but we have a hard time recognizing it in ourselves.[‡] What my son *did* hear was a dad who was confident of his own righteous driving and looked down on the driving of others—a Pharisee on wheels.

My windshield magnifies the highway hijinks of others. I have big windows on every side of the car, and they show every vehicle out there but my own. I have a tiny little mirror that shows me.

You may be a Pharisee if …

- **you catch yourself celebrating someone else's failure.**

- **you obsess over the opinions of others.**

- **you're utterly convinced that your own opinion is the only right one,** that your efforts deserve the most credit, that your tastes are the correct

---

† I'm just kidding, but statistically speaking …

‡ Ma'am in the white Honda Pilot on Westport Road this past Tuesday, this is not an admission of guilt. Next time use your blinker.

ones, that you're the one who should be talking,
that everyone else should be listening.

There just might be a tiny but very persuasive Pharisee inside
you somewhere.

Join the crowd. Pride is the ultimate issue of the human
condition—not just one of the "deadly sins" but the mother of them
all. The Pharisee keeps getting in, no matter how often you shoo him
out. The problem is that we feed him, we let him grow, we let him
give the public prayer, and pretty soon he's running the show. It takes
constant vigilance, and if you do a good job of *that*, you might now
have another topic for pride.

Why is your inner Pharisee so powerful?

Pharisees Get Things Done

The key to understanding your inner Pharisee is that he is all about
performance. That's, of course, the part of us that others see: what
we actually do. We tend to focus on appearances. It's basic human
nature, and the Pharisee is the master of that. If he can make life into
a righteousness tournament, that's a game he can win, because he
knows the rules the way some people know 1927 Yankees baseball
statistics.

So he stresses religion based on following the rules and getting
things done. Fasting and then blogging about it. Giving big bucks
and making the signature on the check extra large. Giving a "testimony." Pharisees love giving a testimony almost as much as they love
the Internet. When your identity is wrapped around what others

think about you, your faith has to be something that happens in plain sight, so nobody misses a single pious act.

In Matthew 23:5, Jesus is talking about spiritual leaders of this type. He says, "Everything they do is done for other people to see." That's the best definition I know of the Pharisee life. One of the central themes of Jesus's sermon is that God looks on the heart, the true measure of who we are. Performance is too easy to fake.

Here's the great danger of performance-based faith. Once we begin to receive those rounds of public applause for all our wonderful accomplishments, we start to believe the charade. We replace the heart with the hands.

Bible-time Pharisees were so good with rules and pious acts that they became legends in their own minds. Yet it wasn't real. The Messiah stood before them, invisible to their eyes. The needs of the hungry and the sick, all around them, didn't register. The things they cared about didn't intersect with the things God cares about.

People loved and admired the Pharisees, so the Pharisees loved and admired themselves. They bought their own hype and missed the greatest miracle in human history.

Again, it's easy to slam the religious leaders of the first century—until we make the appropriate translations and figure out how it all fits into our culture. We tend to hype ourselves through social media. Now, of course, I'm stepping on my own toes, which is an awkward physical position, by the way.

Social media is designed to show us at our best. It's a form of self-publicity, and we tend to post only what we really want others to see. Therefore, as we scroll down the feed in Facebook, we see idealized versions of everyone we know. Then, because of human pride, we're tempted to do exactly the same. It's nearly impossible to promote humility through social media. As a matter of fact, we've come up with a new concept called "the humblebrag" when people attempt to do this.

A humblebrag, according to a new book on the subject, is the practice of the art of false modesty. For instance, a businessman Tweets this one:

> Just filed my taxes. They were right, mo money mo problems.

Or a young lady produces this status update:

> I hate when I go into a store to get something to eat and the male staff are too busy hitting on me to get my order right :(so annoying!

Or a mother creatively praises her own parenting:

> My perfect little princess brought me breakfast in bed again. So much for watching what I eat today. Oh well …

Sure, those are blatant attempts that fail at subtlety as they try to drop in a little boast. But how often do we post about being exhausted after our wild and crazy vacation, pretending the key word is the humble *exhausted* but actually caring more that people note we had a big-time vacation?

I'm hoping I've avoided the humblebrag, but I know my social media likely sounds like that to most people. Of course I'm going to include only what I want people to hear.

I introduced myself to an out-of-town guest at our church recently. We'd never met before, and he said, "Hey, I feel like I know you because I follow you on Facebook and Twitter." Immediately, this struck me as funny. I thought, *You know only what I want you to know about me.* You see the danger? Without even thinking about it, we stand in front of as many people as possible and make much of ourselves.

Comparisons

Who are your models? Who do you measure yourself against? If you're interested in becoming a better person or better at your job, you "compare up." You look for someone who inspires you, someone who could teach you a thing or two. If you had a pride thing, that wouldn't happen. You would compare, sure—you'd always be comparing—but you would compare yourself to people who made you feel better about yourself. Pride is best buddies with insecurity.

The Pharisee in the story from Luke 18 compares down because he wants God to see him in the best possible light. He doesn't look to other spiritual leaders or the prophets of old. He compares himself to the lowest available strata on the social spectrum, the guy others place just above the cockroach. While he's at it, he offers a list of human rejects who don't happen to be in the room—"robbers, evildoers, adulterers"—and, having assembled this roll call of infamy, he figures he stacks up pretty good.

It speaks volumes that the substance of this man's prayer is comparison, which really isn't a typical part of prayer at all. It's how the Pharisee thinks. Since it's all about performance, he evaluates himself by the worst performances imaginable, leaving himself to shine.

It's very American to keep track of comparisons. It's also a trap. Once again, in social media, we're set up to see an ongoing feed of how well and prosperous and happy everybody else is. And we upgrade our online images to keep up.

One way we do this is by downloading a photo filter app to make sure everyone sees the best version of us. As a matter of fact, "real" pictures are so rare that some have taken to adding a #nofilter hashtag to point out we actually posted something as it came out of the camera.

Even then, chances are the #nofilter pic is the best one we've taken in the last year. And what is that hashtag but another form of boasting?

Pride: you can run, but you cannot hide.

An "I" Problem

The greatest danger in life is anything other than Jesus that becomes a foundation for our confidence. Performance-based religion is the false foundation of choice for many of us who grew up in the church.

We find it difficult to talk about our faith without talking about what we do for God, as the Pharisee does. We may not offer the same prayer he did, but we tend to have a righteousness résumé available on a moment's notice. It's just so easy to point to what we do, to stuff on the outside. But Jesus is interested in who we are on the inside, where only he can see, where it is what it is and nothing can be faked.

Four times the Pharisee uses the first-person pronoun *I.* "*I* thank you that *I* am not like other people.... *I* fast twice a week and give a tenth of all *I* get" (Luke 18:11–12). If there's a pride index, it's the number of times you use first-person pronouns per hundred words.

Leviticus 16 recommends fasting one day annually, as required by God's Law. Our Pharisee fasts twice a week. That's more than one hundred times what God asks! But is God really keeping score that way? Is there something like a batting championship for days fasting? Not if it's not from the heart.

Warren Wiersbe writes,

> The great sin of the Pharisees was hypocrisy based on pride. Their religion was external, not internal; it was to impress people, not to please God. They bound people with heavy burdens, while Christ came to set people free (Luke 4:18–19). They loved titles and public recognition and exalted themselves at the expense of others.[1]

Meanwhile, Across the Room

In the parable, we move from the prayer of the Pharisee to the prayer of his archenemy, the tax collector. While the Pharisee is full of himself, the tax collector is at the end of himself.

You can hear it in his prayer: "God, have mercy on me, a sinner" (Luke 18:13). It's fascinating how Jesus details the body language.

Whereas the Pharisee stands and draws attention to himself, this man stands "at a distance." When you're putting on a show, you never stand at a distance.

Then we read that the tax collector wouldn't even look up to heaven. What does that tell us? He's in touch with his unworthiness before God. We also hear that he "beat his breast." It's not lip service; he's not going through the motions. This man is mourning his sin. And his prayer is no more than a few words, but those words offer a picture of humility, of prayer from the inside out. This man has come to the temple for a real encounter with God, and no one else matters. He stands off to himself and has the powerful experience of a man who knows just who he is and just who God is. His prayer is really something of an ordeal.

As we've seen, Jesus offers a blessing to the humble in Matthew 5, as part of the Beatitudes. A chapter later the sermon continues, and Jesus discusses what kind of prayer God loves. Here's a paraphrase of what he says, taken from *The Message*:

> And when you come before God, don't turn that into a theatrical production either. All these people making a regular show out of their prayers, hoping for stardom! Do you think God sits in a box seat? Here's what I want you to do: Find a quiet, secluded place so you won't be tempted to role-play before God. Just be there as simply and honestly as you can manage. The focus will shift from you to God, and you will begin to sense his grace. (Matt. 6:5–6)

The Pharisee thinks all the world's a stage and he is the player performing to God's admiring applause. Not only does he follow the rules, but he actually adds new ones. He is a righteousness overachiever, scrambling up the ladder and pushing off everyone in his way.

Yet God is not impressed. He wants us to *sit* in his theater and to behold his glory because there is no other glory. The tax collector understands. He shows us what "the end of me" looks like. He is broken, humbled by the majesty of God, and all he can do is plead for mercy and grace as he acknowledges the toll of sin in his life.

As Jesus finishes his story, he gives out the grades. The religious expert gets an F, and the stammering wretch gets an A. The tax collector, whose prayer was an ordeal, "rather than the other, went home justified before God. For all those who exalt themselves will be humbled, and those who humble themselves will be exalted" (Luke 18:14).

Once again, he has turned our expectations upside down.

To-Do List, To-Don't List

There are things you learn in the work of ministry. One is that people come to church looking for solutions. They're caught up in their problems, and they wonder if there could be a supernatural answer. Debt, addiction, a failing marriage—whatever it is, sooner or later they ask for action steps. Bullet points, in careful order, for resolving the problem. "What can I do?" We always assume the answer is in the word *do*.

And while sometimes we have some dos that need to get done, the truth is there's no substitute for humbling ourselves. At this point someone says, "Sure, I get it. Be more humble. But there's got to be something I can, you know, *do*. Other than be more humble."

It's so much easier to *do* than to *be*. *To do* is to take some action. *To be* requires real transformation.

You want to know what to do? Fine, we can do it that way.

- Stand at a distance.
- Beat your chest.
- Pray this: "God, have mercy on me."
- Mean it.

I'm going to go out on a limb and say that last one is the key. It happens when you humble yourself.

Are you interested in some *don'ts*?

- Don't make your case.
- Don't pull out your résumé.
- Don't ask for blessings by comparing yourself to others.
- Don't tell God all the reasons you deserve to be blessed.
- Don't congratulate God for having you as a child.
- Don't thank God for all the hard work you've put in.

There is no substitute for humbling yourself before God. The humble heart pleases God. The humble cry invites him to demonstrate his power. Was Jesus really saying something new? Actually the

Scriptures spoke early and often about that: Psalm 18:27 says, "You save the humble but bring low those whose eyes are haughty." Proverbs 3:34 says, "He mocks proud mockers but shows favor to the humble and oppressed." And in Isaiah 66:2, God said, "These are the ones I look on with favor: those who are humble and contrite in spirit."

In the Sermon on the Mount, Jesus is underlining a truth established from the beginning. It seems like a reversal only because we have turned things in the wrong direction.

Humble Myself

Don't miss these four words of Jesus from the end of the parable of the Pharisee and the tax collector: "those who humble themselves" (Luke 18:14).

Being humbled is something we think of as a passive activity—that is, somebody or something humbles us. We are humbled by unemployment, by a failed relationship, by a dream shattered. But Jesus speaks of a humbling that is *active*—we are the humblers. This is not something we wait for to occur naturally. "Humble yourself." It doesn't sound right, does it? Almost a little masochistic. We're used to being advised to assert ourselves, not to humble ourselves.

Nik Wallenda got huge TV ratings a few years ago. He walked across Niagara Falls on a high wire in 2012. Then in 2013, he became the first man to walk a wire across the Grand Canyon. Knowing he's a strong Christian, I wondered how he handled the problem of pride. How do you humble yourself when you're the best in the world at something and millions tune in to cheer your every step?

I'll tell you how. Huge crowds come to these events, and they leave huge loads of garbage in their wake. After his walk, Wallenda didn't head for a limousine. He spent hours walking around, picking up the trash his fans had strewn. He said:

> Three hours of cleaning up debris is good for my soul. Humility does not come naturally to me. So if I have to force myself into situations that are humbling, so be it.... I do it ... because it's a way to keep from tripping. As a follower of Jesus, I see Him washing the feet of others. I do it because if I don't serve others I'll be serving nothing but my ego.[2]

Even if you're not a high-wire walker, pride goes before a fall (see Prov. 16:18).

And what's the absolute opposite, the ultimate answer for the pride problem? Jesus shows us in Philippians 2.

> Being in very nature God, [Jesus] did not consider equality with God something to be used to his own advantage; rather, he made himself nothing by taking the very nature of a servant, being made in human likeness. And being found in appearance as a man, he humbled himself by becoming obedient to death—even death on a cross! (vv. 6–8)

This is the masterwork of humility—what Christ did. He made himself nothing. He humbled himself. This was someone who was in very nature—in very essence—God, but who didn't cling to that status; rather, he made himself nothing.

And there it is again: taking ownership of our own humility. Getting it done. But how? What does it look like? How can we humble ourselves without becoming proud of our humility and wrecking the whole thing?

All I can offer you is a list of ideas I've found helpful. You can add to this list, I'm certain, but here's what helps me get to the end of me:

- **To humble myself, I voluntarily confess sin.**

    If I confess because I got caught, I'm humbled—but I'm not humbling myself. If I confess because I'm confronted, I'm humbled—but I'm not humbling myself. Voluntary confession is a way of humbling myself, and God exalts those who do it. That's his promise. The alternative is to keep putting up a front. I can keep up my act and exalt myself. That has a promise attached to it as well: I will be humbled. So why not go ahead and take ownership?

- **To humble myself, I give sacrificially and anonymously.**

    When I give anonymously, so I can't be thanked or exalted by others, my heart stays humble. When I give sacrificially, meaning it costs me something, it's a very real way of saying the kingdom of God is more important than me. It reminds me I'm not the most important person in my life.

• **To humble myself, I treat others better than myself.**

In Philippians 2:3, Paul wrote, "In humility value others above yourselves." It's the modern way, turned on its ear. We're taught to be self-reliant and look out for number one, but what if I placed a higher value on others than myself? Maybe my friend would pick the restaurant. Maybe how I listen to my spouse would change. Maybe I wouldn't complain when a family member asked me for help. Maybe I wouldn't fight for the front seat, or the biggest piece, or the best view, or the most recognition. If I want to humble myself, I find someone most people would place beneath me in the pecking order—and create a great reversal of that.

• **To humble myself, I ask for help.**

It's humbling to say to someone, "Here's the mess I've gotten myself into," or "I don't know what to do. I need help." Guys struggle with this one. We don't even like reading the instructions or stopping to ask directions. But I've found that every time I humble myself and ask for help, it opens a new door to some kind of blessing.

I challenge you to improve on what I've offered here. Be creative. Remember that humbling yourself is not beating yourself up or believing that you should be treated poorly. Where are your opportunities to humble yourself? Before moving on to the next chapter, take some time to write down a few starting points for yourself. Put them someplace where you'll see them and be reminded.

No doubt there's a vast frontier of strategies for humbling ourselves yet to be claimed simply because so few have gone there. Everywhere you look, every situation you're in, is a laboratory for self-humbling, an opportunity to exalt Christ and put pride on the cross. You can boldly—or humbly—go where no one has gone before.

Chapter 4

Authentic to Be Accepted

When my grandfather died, I went home for the funeral. I took with me some dress slacks that I needed to have cleaned for the visitation. Driving around, I found a place called One Hour Cleaners. That sounded perfect because I needed those slacks that very evening.

I walked in with my laundry on a coat hanger and smiled at the woman behind the counter. "I'm from out of town, and I'm really glad to find this place," I said. "One Hour Cleaners, right?"

"Yes, sir. That's us."

"Just to make sure we're on the same page, you can do these pants, right?"

"Of course we can. Yes, sir."

"So I can leave them with you right now. Then I can go get some other things done, then come pick them up in an hour or so, right?"

"No, sir," she said, squinting as if I'd said something odd. "But you can pick them up tomorrow."

"Um, but your sign says One Hour Cleaners." I pointed through the window to substantiate my charge.

She chomped her chewing gum a few times, then said, "Yeah, but we don't clean clothes in one hour."

"Then shouldn't this business be called Next Day Cleaners? Or Whenever It's Done Cleaners?"

She just chewed her gum and squinted at me. Clearly this was a strange new request by a customer. Laundry back in an hour from One Hour Cleaners? What will they be demanding next?

I tried discussing it with her, always politely, from several angles, hoping we could at least enjoy the irony of it together. But she saw nothing remarkable about the situation. I wanted to say, "I don't think those words mean what you think they mean." This was my hometown. Maybe I'd been away too long and the language had evolved beyond my understanding in these parts.

Or maybe it was just another case of false advertising. Nobody likes it when someone advertises one thing and delivers another—commercially or otherwise. The outside of the establishment should give us an accurate expectation of what we'll find on the inside.

Then again, once we apply this to ourselves, it's a little different. It's one thing to talk about businesses with false claims. It's another to look in the mirror and ask whether we really show the world exactly who we are.

We struggle with authenticity because we fear rejection. We want the world to see us at our very best, because then people are more likely to accept and possibly even admire us.

Maybe we don't need to try so hard or hide any of our blemishes. Maybe people will like us just the way we are. It's even possible they'll be *more* drawn to us if they know some of our failings and struggles. They could say, "I'm like that too. I have the same issues. I'm glad to know there are two of us."

But that's a risk we won't take. Fear is the enemy of transparency. We don't like our flaws, and we don't expect anybody else to. So we work hard at putting up the most impressive front we can.

Then we come back to that sermon Jesus preached on the mountainside. Before moving on from the Beatitudes, let's examine one more of these upside-down blessings.

Jesus has been telling us that the kingdom of God is in favor of the ones at the bottom of the heap, the ones who are last instead of first; the poor in spirit, not the arrogant and powerful; the meek and gentle, not the pushy and overbearing.

In that sermon, Jesus actually has a lot to say about the difference between the outside and the inside. He says what really matters to God is what's inside, where we transact our real business.

He says people spend a lot of time working on their signage for the world to see, but God comes right in to see what our true policies are.

Jesus puts it this way:

Blessed are the pure in heart, for they will see God. (Matt. 5:8)

Pure in heart. That's something to think about, isn't it? It means you're living the blessed life when you stop worrying about the signs and the extravagant advertising and all the effort expended trying to convince people you're something different than you are. When the inside and outside match up, you're pure in heart and you're where he wants you to be.

Getting to the end of me means I'm not worried about performing for others anymore. Getting to the end of me means I'm no longer interested in faking it, because I understand that God is looking for the real me.

Pure and Unmixed

What does it mean to have a pure heart?

As soon as Jesus spoke this word *pure*, bells and buzzers sounded for those listening. If any one word captured what religion was all about in that culture, it was *purity*. To be pure was to be clean and not infected with the wrong things. But the Pharisees and other religious leaders defined it almost completely in terms of things other people could see. It had become a matter of keeping so many rules. You don't eat certain foods, as everyone had known since the earliest days of Israel, when God gave Moses the laws. "Unclean" food made *you* unclean.

That was long established. But you also didn't eat with "unclean" people, meaning Gentiles. That also made you unclean. But Jesus did that all the time.

The Pharisees took tremendous pains to show they were pure, and they also took tremendous pains to make sure others did the same. But Jesus was challenging their entire concept of what was pure and clean. At one point, in Matthew 23, he told them they were too worried about cleaning "the outside of the cup" (v. 25) while the inside was filthy. Then—and you know this one wasn't too popular—he compared them, the leaders, to "whitewashed tombs," which were sparkling and bright on the outside but filled with death and decay on the inside (v. 27).

Pretty harsh words, but they illustrated where Jesus thought it most important to be clean and pure. Painting and exteriors are nice, but it's the interior that counts. A great part of the upside-down, inside-out message of Jesus is that God doesn't look so much on the outside, which is so easy to fake. He looks more on the inside, where we are what we are.

So Jesus drops the well-worn word *pure* into his sermon and then gives it a dramatic new spin. People need to stop worrying about their outward appearance and realize that God sees inside us. Purity of heart over purity of decoration.

As for the word *purity* itself, there are two words that capture what it means. First of all it means *unmixed*: no bad ingredients thrown in.

When I was in grade school, we had a game in our neighborhood. We'd raid the pantry and find all kinds of food to mix in a blender. We'd put in eggs, peanut butter, ketchup, mustard, cottage cheese, and anything else we could get our hands on. Surprisingly enough, my mother was okay with this, as long as we followed two rules:

1. Everything we put into the blender had to be edible. No dirt, rocks, or metal. Items like shaving cream fell into the gray area.

2. We had to eat one spoonful of the final concoction.

That's why this game quickly lost its appeal. We got results that looked and smelled awful, and tasted even worse.

Sometimes I wonder if my heart resembles our blender game. It's certainly not pure and unmixed. What about you? What ingredients have you poured into the blender of your heart?

The New Testament has a lot to say about the kinds of things we put inside us. For example, Paul tells us, "Whatever is true, whatever is noble, whatever is right, whatever is pure, whatever is lovely, whatever is admirable—if anything is excellent or praiseworthy—think about such things" (Phil. 4:8). When you pour in the right ingredients and avoid the others, you find it's a recipe that pleases God. Proverbs 11:20 says, "The LORD detests people with crooked hearts, but he delights in those with integrity" (NLT).

Sincere

We also might use the word *sincere* to describe a pure heart.

When Jesus speaks of a pure heart, he's talking about one that is honest and has no little ugly places hidden within it.

In Matthew 5, as we've already discussed, Jesus begins his ministry by offering us a list of blessings, which we call the Beatitudes. But he ends his ministry by offering a list of "woes" in Matthew 23. This includes the references to cups and whitewashed tombs previously mentioned. At this point, the time for his arrest is drawing near and he knows he has only a few days left on earth. He is preaching in the temple, and he aims his message squarely at the Pharisees and their hypocrisy by saying, "Everything they do is done for people to see" (v. 5). Hypocrisy is the opposite of sincerity.

Jesus also quotes Isaiah, saying of the hypocrites, "These people honor me with their lips, but their hearts are far from me" (Matt. 15:8).

So don't miss this. Jesus begins his ministry by saying, "Blessed are the pure in heart." He ends it by saying, "Woe to you, … you hypocrites!" The word *woe*, of course, is the opposite of *blessed*. It's also an expression of grief. Jesus is telling us that the best things come from God to those who have pure hearts, unmixed and sincere; the worst things come to those who play the blender game.

Earning Our Stars

Jesus says more about purity of heart in Matthew 6:

> Be careful not to practice your righteousness in front
> of others to be seen by them. If you do, you will have
> no reward from your Father in heaven. (v. 1)

In the kingdom economy, a lot is determined by the audience you choose. If you're most interested in what other people think, then their applause or attention is your reward. If they say you're a tremendous human being, then that's your reward. You've been paid in full, and you shouldn't look for any further commendation from God.

But coming to the end of me means I am through with that charade and the emptiness of it. Instead, I seek only to please God—I receive my reward from him instead of from people. When we close the public theater, drop the curtains, shut off the lights, and play to an audience of one, not caring about the reviews of the critics or anyone else, that's when we come to the end of ourselves and experience God's blessing.

I attended Sunday school every week when I was growing up. I remember how our classroom had a sticker chart that allowed the teacher to keep track of all the leading indicators of Sunday school excellence. You got a sticker for coming to church, for instance. You got another one for bringing a Bible, and yet another for bringing a little envelope with an offering in it. If you brought a friend with you, that was worth another sticker.

It was just a little sticky star, and it bought me no candy or free prizes or anything else apart from credit on the wall poster. Even so, there was something motivational about seeing the stars on my poster. People are naturally competitive, and if you put the names of all the kids together and create "standings," we start trying to win. It's human nature.

I remember trying to get those stars and beginning to define my faith by whether my Bible was in my hand and whether the offering envelope was sticking out of my Bible. If we missed church, that was a whole row of stars I lost out on for the day. So it was an effective strategy for teaching us good habits. The problem comes when we metabolize a habit into a philosophy and come to believe that our faith is defined by things we do with no reference to the heart.

Even as adults, we look around at other people and mentally give—or don't give—them stickers. Maybe that guy over there brought his ragged Bible from childhood rather than the cool translation of the day in the nice embroidered cover, so you mentally dock him a star for that. That lady over there attends a home Bible study group, so she gets an extra star. We evaluate others by their outside signage.

Jesus criticized the religious leaders because they were consumed by appearances. "Everything they do is done for people to see" (Matt. 23:5). Jesus had a lot to say about how the Pharisees made great public performances out of praying and fasting. They painted their faces, they doused themselves in ashes, and they made sure everyone saw their shows of righteousness. It seems to us that it must have been an odd sight to see the street performance art of the religious leaders. But I wonder if we do the same thing.

When we bow to give thanks in a restaurant, how unmixed and sincere are our hearts? Are we thinking entirely about God and his provision of the meal, or is some part of us thinking about how we appear to others present?

When we raise our hand to volunteer for a project at church, how much of the heart is allocated to pleasing God, and how much is concerned with who is watching and how impressed they may be?

Do we wonder who's watching us as the offering plate goes by?

When we stand to pray publicly, are the words geared to God's ear or to those listening?

#lookatme

In the last chapter I mentioned that social media can contribute to our tendency to be too concerned with what others think. I want to unpack that idea a little more, but first I want to make sure you understand that I'm not anti–social media. I think it can serve a valuable purpose, but here's what I've observed. Social media is about the control of appearances. I believe Facebook, Twitter, and the rest can be very useful to God's kingdom, but we need to be thinking and praying about social media, because it really plays to our preoccupations with the opinions of others.

Let's say you go on a vacation with your family. There are certain things you post and certain things you don't. Picture of happy family on beach?† Post it! Fighting in the car on the way to the beach? That one never appears on Instagram.

You post, "Date night with hubby!" and with it, a picture of the two of you gazing lovingly into each other's eyes. And of course you add a humble caption about marrying way up.

Nobody posts that Monday morning picture: two grumpy people, snarling—her with hair in curlers, him with shaving cuts—and needing a little space from each other.

So many of the people behind these idyllic social media identities actually need prayer rather than quick love bombs: for bills they can't pay, conflicts they can't soften, and family members they're worried about. We don't intend dishonesty. We're simply being positive people who want to share our lives and our work. But the screen on the phone or computer seems to lend itself to performance over transparency.

It used to be that family Christmas letters were the great repository of public posturing. "Here's a picture of our happy, laughing family and an account of our incredible accomplishments during the year—written from the point of view of our adorable puppy!"

Those letters are still sent out, but today we're shifting more to social media, which is like a little stream of "happy-talk Christmas letter" self-promotion all through the year. If we become consumed by Tweeting out messages, it changes our focus. We're now putting a great deal of time into practicing our righteousness before the world.

†   Wearing khakis and white shirts? I thought so.

I think the Pharisees would have had huge followings on Twitter. People would have cheered them on as they fasted and pointed out that this was their five thousandth straight day without a violation of the Mosaic Law. "Love you all!" folks would comment. "Great job chastising those lepers! Wish I'd been there!"

Another Pharisee would post, "I'm live-blogging my weeping and wailing. Don't forget to leave comments!" And others would cheer him on, which of course doesn't much enhance weeping and wailing.

I saw a T-shirt I liked. It said, "May your life someday be as awesome as you make it appear to be on Facebook." How important is our appearance on social media to us? And what does that say about purity of heart?

Maybe it's a good thing if it accelerates the process of burning us out on performance—of bringing us closer to the end of ourselves. It's exhausting trying to play a part. Writing before the advent of social media, John Stott observed,

> Yet how few of us live one life and live it in the open! We are tempted to wear a different mask and play a different role according to each occasion. This is not reality but play-acting, which is the essence of hypocrisy. Some people weave round themselves such a tissue of lies that they can no longer tell which part of them is real and which is make-believe.[1]

Jesus calls us to live one life and live it out in the open. His name for that is purity of heart, and his reward for that is a rich and fulfilling blessing in life.

Faith and High Fashion

Hypocrites are the opposite of those who are pure in heart. Jesus wanted his people to demonstrate through their lives the power and grace of God, but the leaders turned it into a cheap form of theater that called attention to the actor.

The religious leaders judged the inside by the outside. If you played by the right rules, it meant you were godly and worthy to pass their test. They even measured faith by the choice of clothing. Listen to Jesus:

> Everything they do is done for people to see: They make their phylacteries wide and the tassels on their garments long. (Matt. 23:5)

Phylacteries were leather boxes containing bits of parchment inscribed with Scripture verses. It was a response to the Old Testament verses, found in Deuteronomy, about binding God's Word to one's arms and foreheads. The real meaning, of course, is for us to bury his Word in our hearts so we can carry it with us everywhere we go.

But the leaders decided this was something to practice in the literal sense. So they wore two black boxes, one on the forehead and the other on the left arm. As you can imagine, once that was established, there was a gradual trend toward bigger boxes to show bigger righteousness. As in, "Now, *there's* a righteous Pharisee—look at the size of the black box on his forehead!"

Then came "the tassels on their garments." The Old Testament referred to garments having a border with a blue ribbon. Again, the Pharisees decided wider ribbons would make a broader statement.

The Pharisees were all about signage. If neon had been invented, they would have worked it into their garb—maybe blinking neon arrows that said, "God likes this guy!"

Some people still believe God is deeply concerned about their Sunday best when they dress for church. "I'm dressing for God," they say, "so I'm going to wear my very best clothing." And there's nothing wrong with that—as long as we're truly unconcerned about others being impressed with a new suit or dress and as long as we recall that "people look at the outward appearance, but the LORD looks at the heart" (1 Sam. 16:7).

He wants authenticity in our worship, our relationships, and in everything about us—one life lived out in the open. Woe to you, Jesus says, if you equate outward appearance with eternal standing. Woe to you if you judge someone's faith by your own sense of style. Woe to you for turning the walk of faith into a red-carpet fashion show. And woe to you if you spend more time primping for church than you do in prayer and seeking to know him better.

I've been on many airline flights, but only once in first class. And that was one time too many. Once you've been up behind the curtain, in the flight version of the Holy of Holies, then coach class loses all its appeal.

On my one encounter, I was on an overbooked flight. Some of us were moved to first class just to fit everyone on the plane. I was pleased, to say the least. As people filed by on their way to coach—the huddled masses—I tried to give them sympathetic looks. I'd received my share of those in the past. Then, instead of studying my message for the speaking engagement ahead of me, I began looking around to figure out who didn't belong up there.

To be honest, I didn't think most of them should be among us elite. One guy had an earring, long hair, and tattoos. I felt disrespected. And when a guy took off his shoes midflight, revealing a hole in his sock, I could only shake my head. And I won't talk about the woman who used poor manners while eating, right down to asking if she could have the can with her drink. Four out of five of those people just weren't first-class material. There are standards, you know.

Worrying about appearances has that effect on us. I ran into a friend at a show in downtown Louisville a few years ago, and we stood in the aisle and chatted. He had pretty long hair;[†] he was fairly grungy, actually. This was on a Saturday night, and the next morning at church, a group of people stopped me in the lobby. They'd seen me on the previous night at the show, and one of them said, "We saw you talking to that rough-looking young man. We were all proud of you for having friends like that, and we prayed for the young man."

For a moment I couldn't figure out what they were talking about. Then, as I walked away, I realized they meant my long-haired, grungy friend—who happened to be none other than the worship leader for our college ministry, and also, ironically, one of the most pure-hearted and humble men I've been around. But on account of his appearance, these folks were praying for his lost soul.

Some would argue that dress is a way to honor tradition, which is important. And that's fine, but notice that this was actually one of Jesus's criticisms of the religious leaders. Tradition had become more

---

†   To clarify, I'm not saying his long hair was pretty. I'm saying it was longer than what would typically be thought of as long hair.

important than people. God wants us to open a place of worship that is a hospital for the hurting rather than a first-class compartment for the heaven-bound.

Rehearsing Lines

In Matthew 6 Jesus gives another example of an impure, inauthentic heart.

> When you pray, do not be like the hypocrites, for they love to pray standing in the synagogues and on the street corners to be seen by others.… But when you pray, go into your room, close the door and pray to your Father, who is unseen. Then your Father, who sees what is done in secret, will reward you." (vv. 5–6)

For many of the Jews, prayer had become a formal, lifeless ritual. As one example, they were to recite the *Shema* every morning before nine o'clock and every evening before nine o'clock. It didn't matter where you found yourself at that time of day—at home, on the street, at work. You stopped and said your Shema. It had become an act we would refer to as "vain repetition"—reciting words out of ritual, without really thinking about them.

The second prayer that every Jew had to repeat each day was called the *Shemoneh Esreh,* which means "the eighteen" because it was a group of eighteen prayers. They were to say these scripted prayers three times a day.

The Jews had a special prayer for every occasion. They had prayers before each meal, prayers for the new moon, prayers for receiving good news, prayers for entering or leaving a city. The longer the prayers, the more effective they were, or so people thought. It was a very convenient system, since everything was prewritten. All they had to provide was the mouth.

Jesus saw things differently. He said that when we talk to God, we simply need to be who we are—to be authentic and to talk to him as we would talk to someone we love.

Many of us have struck spiritual poses in our prayers. We have a hard time being ourselves. Praying before others, we have a tendency to talk more to the people in the room than to God. Even in private prayer, sincerity doesn't come easily. We talk to God as if he requires formal language, as we would talk to some governmental authority we didn't know well. Or we speak in a kind of fake biblical language we've cobbled together from the Scriptures or other embellished prayers we've heard. Prayer becomes a performance, and we have to work at it.

God simply wants us to talk with him. Talk is simple communication, and it doesn't need to be dressed up. We should talk to him as we'd talk to a best friend—simply being ourselves, being totally honest without worrying how it might sound.

Have you ever listened to a public prayer and really liked a turn of phrase? And you thought to yourself, *That's awesome—I'm going to put that into my prayer repertoire!* We pick up phrases like these: *traveling mercies; lead, guide, and direct; the nourishment of our bodies.* Perhaps we believe those are special phrases that establish some kind of spiritual superiority. But it's not God's language. He wants to hear from the real me and the real you.

Who we're pretending to be doesn't match who we are on the inside. Yet what he asks could not be simpler. His invitation says, "Come as you are. Please don't dress up. Don't decorate your language. Don't put on a show. Just be at home with me. Be real. My place is your place."

Our ingrained mask-wearing keeps us from having the authentic, intimate relationship that Jesus wants to have with us. What if you put on this kind of show with your spouse, dressing things up and trying to be someone you aren't? A wife would feel she needed to be in her finest clothing with all her cosmetics on at every single moment. A husband would believe he had to put on a show as well. Both would speak to each other as they'd speak to someone on a first date, dancing around things, worried about saying the wrong words. Marriage would be totally exhausting and utterly unsatisfying. After a few weeks of it we'd be hiding from each other.

What we love in marriage is the utter relaxation, the complete intimacy we enjoy with each other. We let down our hair, we stop hiding our warts, and we say whatever is on our minds. Why can't we be that way with God?

Getting to the end of me means I don't need to hide my flaws because I know his love is unconditional. And we'll be deeply satisfied, deeply fulfilled, because it's so much easier to be one person than two—so much easier not to create and sustain a false identity.

My relationship with my wife became more intimate the first time I saw her without makeup, with her hair pulled back in a ponytail. At that point, we were a little more comfortable with each other. We were starting to relax and say what we thought. That's when it became a true relationship rather than an audition.

Sometimes, on date nights, it's still fun to get dressed up and go somewhere that requires perfect manners. But my wife is most beautiful to me in jeans and a sweatshirt, with her hair pulled back, because then I know I'm seeing her at her most relaxed, her most completely authentic self.

Jesus wants a no-makeup relationship with you. He wants you to be pure in heart—unmixed and soul-sincere.

Exit Stage

Jesus says in Matthew 23:3 that hypocrites "do not practice what they preach."

This week I watched an old TV show called *Faking It* on the Internet. This show was built around the premise of training a person to be something he or she really wasn't. For example, on one episode a guy named Patrick Nesbitt was a very comfortable real estate developer in LA. But he spent a month training to work on a western ranch as a cowboy.

Another contestant was Lesley Townsend, a self-confessed geek who enjoyed books more than people. The show transformed her into a perky NFL cheerleader. And David Dougherty was a carpenter from a small eastern town. On *Faking It,* he became a Beverly Hills interior designer.

These guests all learned their roles, then lined up against people who were authentic at those careers. Professional judges had to spot the imposter. Who was the real cowboy? The real cheerleader? The real interior designer? I had to admit it was fun watching these people doing their best to fake it, but I got tired watching all their exertion.

As I watched the show, I wondered how many people I know live this way. How many are exhausting themselves trying to be something they really aren't?

That's not a blessed life but a miserable one. Woe unto those who play the game, trying to inflate their reputations by being someone they're not. They will ultimately collapse from sheer exhaustion, their pretenses collapsing with them.

You need to understand that I'm writing this as a memo to myself as well as to anyone else. I don't try to fake it; nobody does. But it's so easy for me put on a show, add a little extra, be more than I am. Every instinct I have tells me to cover my sin deeply, to stamp a big smile across my face, and to give the impression that I have all the answers. But getting to the end of me means getting over myself so the real me can experience the real life available in Christ.

Clean Hands, Pure Heart

"If we confess our sins, he is faithful and just and will forgive us our sins and *purify* us from all unrighteousness" (1 John 1:9, emphasis mine).

If you want to have a pure heart, do something about the impurities. Don't have a mixed heart. Be sincere, with God and with other people, and he promises to purify and clean you.

In the Bible there is a special connection between clean hands and a pure heart. In Psalm 24:3–4 we read, "Who may ascend the mountain of the LORD? Who may stand in his holy place? The one who has clean hands and a pure heart."

Then we read, "Come near to God and he will come near to you. Wash your hands, you sinners, and purify your hearts" (James 4:8).

In the Old Testament, washing your hands wasn't just something you did before dinner. It was a symbol of spiritual cleansing. When Solomon was building the temple to honor God, he had five washbasins placed on the south side of the temple and five on the north side. Before entering the temple, people would stop and wash their hands as a reminder that they were cleansing their spirits in preparation for worship. We want to come before God as ourselves, unmasked, with all impurities out of the way.

As you finish this chapter, I suggest something a little unusual. Go to a sink and take a moment to wash your hands. As you see the water trickle through your fingers, cleansing away the simple impurities, ask God to cleanse your heart, to show you where you can be more authentic. You can do a good job washing the outside, but nobody but God can cleanse the interior.

The Bible's promise to you is that as your heart becomes pure, you will receive the most incredible blessing: you will see God. The real you will know the real him. The relationship will not be based on performance and pretense but will be authentic. I can't think of a greater blessing than seeing God. To authentically know him and to be authentically known by him is what my soul was made for.

He will see you—just as you are, without the pretense, without the performance—and you will see him. Can you imagine a better offer than that?

Part 2
_____

Where Strength Begins

Chapter 5

Empty to Be Filled

I read a story about a single mother who was in a very tough spot. As we all know, single moms have one of the most grueling and thankless jobs on the planet. Quite a number of them are among my personal heroes.

One had an especially compelling story. She was not only a single mom but also a recent widow. Her husband had been a godly man whom everyone admired. When he passed away, he left a loving wife and two sons. He also left a mountain of debt and no life insurance.

The woman had no real way to work, and her sons were still young, so she found herself a pauper overnight. She had debts she simply couldn't pay, and where she lived, debtors weren't treated well. Cash was tight for everyone, so there was no mercy.

The widow was staring down the possibility of her two sons being sold into slavery until the mortgage was paid. In her culture, that kind of thing happened all the time.

She cried until she was empty of tears. She had nothing left but desperation. This widowed mother was at the end of herself, and she was down to one not-so-promising idea. She would go visit the preacher. After all, her husband had worked in this man's ministry. They'd had a good relationship. Maybe he would feel some loyalty and help her find some kind of financial solution.

"I'm at my wit's end," she told the preacher. "We've already lost everything, and my boys are all I have now. But they'll be gone, and the house, too, if I don't come up with some money fast. My boys will die in slavery, without my ever seeing them again, and I'll be in a gutter begging for coins—or worse. You know how my husband loved and served the Lord. The two of you ministered shoulder to shoulder. Surely God won't look away from us now. Or you?"

The preacher reached over and gently wiped away a few of the woman's tears. "I'm so sorry for what you're going through," he said. "What have you got left?"

She met his gaze, puzzled. Was he actually demanding some kind of payment? "Nothing—I've got nothing, like I said." And she began to cry all over again.

"Nothing but walls and floor?"

"I sold it all. Empty rooms filled with memories and nothing else. I think there's one little flask of olive oil on the shelf. Useless."

The preacher, whose name happened to be Elisha, told her to go door to door, asking her neighbors to lend her any empty jars they could spare. Then, he said, place the jars on the floor and close up the room. Then, get the olive oil and begin pouring.

"How could that possibly help?" asked the widow.

"Have faith," he said and smiled.

Some hours later, the room was filled with jars—and the jars were filled with oil. The boys were laughing as they ran from jar to jar, and the little flask just kept giving and giving. Then the last drop fell, at the rim of the last jar. The three of them began hugging, crying, jumping up and down.

"When you sell the oil," Elisha told her, "I think you'll find your debts paid, and just enough left to live on."

Of course he was right.

What's in Your Jar?

That story, found in 2 Kings 4, is a reminder that God loves to fill empty things—whether it's a jar or a measure of hope. Jars are made for filling. They don't fill themselves, but they receive what is poured into them. All jars begin with emptiness.

It's much the same with you and me. The measure of filling we receive is in direct proportion to our level of emptiness.

It's highly likely there are readers of this chapter who have come to the end of themselves—to the place of emptiness. If that's you, I'm sure it wasn't part of your plan. Life has a way of pouring us out, and it has nothing to do with what we wanted or expected. Life takes away someone we love. It takes away a home. A job. It can reach under the skin and take away our health and our hope. At some point, we're left holding what feels a lot like nothing, and we hold on to it with clenched fists.

We feel a surge of unwanted emotions: Fear. Vulnerability. Loneliness. Anger. Resentment. Ultimately the worst emotional state of all: emptiness itself. We feel nothing; we're done. That's called despair.

But what if that emptiness means God has us right where he wants us?

What would the emotions be if we could perceive one small glimmering truth? We're in position for the most wonderful thing that can happen in life—a close encounter with a loving heavenly Father who has in-depth, sweeping plans for blessing us in ways we never imagined.

When life takes away, God gives. The soothing oil of his incredible love seeps into the aching cavity of a shattered life. Then "You 2.0" can begin.

I also suspect there are more than a few jars out there that are full to the brim. We'd prove it by pointing to our calendars, booked solid. Probably overbooked. The oil of the good life seems to be running over the brim, because we just can't contain all the stuff life has brought us. We'd say it's all good. At Thanksgiving, we sit at the table and talk about how full our lives are, and hours later we talk about how full our stomachs are. Life is loaded, and we thank God for it.

But what if some of that load is counterproductive to the God part of things?

There's nothing wrong with a good job, a loving marriage, and a busy agenda. I'm just wondering what's there that is really significant—things that will matter ten, twenty years from now, when the calendar pages are dust in the wind. How much divine dialogue is going on at the soul level?

I want to explore with you the difference between a jar that is full and a jar that is filled.

Jesus Loves to Fill What's Empty

God is a filler of empty spaces, and Jesus was a living picture of what that means.

In his very first public miracle, recorded in John 2, we find Jesus changing water into wine. It's a wedding party, so it's been carefully planned. But the host receives word from the servants that the wine is running low far too early. In that culture, going dry would be an unforgivable social blunder.

These weddings weren't like our afternoon affairs. A wedding was a seven-day party, and the wine was supposed to last. Running out would expose the host to public ridicule. Once again we have empty jars. Jesus asks for six of them to be filled with water, which he then changes into wine. What John is careful to tell us, however, is that Jesus doesn't fill the jars with just any wine, but the best. The bridegroom is then commended for saving the best wine for last, a rarity at these functions. Jesus doesn't just fill emptiness; he fills it with joy and abundance.

In John 4, Jesus finds a woman by a well. Her life is empty. He fills it.

In John 6, he faces a vast crowd of growling stomachs. He fills them all.

In the home of Jairus, he finds the emptiness of loss, as a daughter has died. Jesus fills the house with joy by bringing her back to life.

He saves a woman caught in adultery and fills her empty days with a hope she has never known.

We could run through every page of the Gospels, and in the whirlwind of people and teachings and miracles, we'd find there is really one story: *Jesus fills.*

Some of the characters we meet, of course, walk away empty. The rich young ruler, for instance, had no room amid his riches. The Pharisees listened carefully to his teaching, but they were too invested in laws and rituals and ideas that could not be cleared away. Emptying is never painless, and not everyone is willing to go there.

Jesus is eager and willing to fill. But someone else has to make the room.

Sunday Dinner

In Luke 14 Jesus tells the parable of the great banquet. It's during one of those meals he often has with religious leaders,[†] which is almost always a sign that things are about to get ~~interesting~~ awkward.

A sick man enters the room during the meal. He probably has edema; his body is filled with excess fluids, but his health is an empty jar. Naturally Jesus fills it and heals the man.

It should be a wonderful moment. There should be tears and laughter all around. But we've already been told that Jesus is being "carefully watched" (v. 1)—almost as if they expect him to steal the silverware. The miracle is met by stony silence.

So Jesus asks them what they think about this healing—you know, happening on the Sabbath and all. He knows what they're thinking.

They sit and stare at him. Perhaps the temperature falls ten degrees in the room; a bit of smoke begins to drift from some of their ears. These men, of course, would have told the man to come back tomorrow; God doesn't like being bothered on days of rest.

We wonder why these faith experts don't begin to question their preconceptions as they see Jesus do these things. After all, his way actually seems to do some dramatic things, while their way is

---

† So we know they weren't eating at Chick-fil-A.

something like a glorified hall monitor catching people out of class. They have no room. They're filled with ideas now chiseled into the stone of their hearts. With all they have, they've bought into Jesus being wrong. So Jesus has to be the enemy, no matter what he teaches or whom he heals.

I wish I could say it was just a Pharisee thing, now defunct. But all of us who attend churches know otherwise. Among many empty jars, open and eager, there are people who aren't really looking to receive anything—at least not the kind of thing Jesus wants to give them. Many of them have actually come to give. But instead of service, love, or compassion, they give criticism. They give a piece of their minds. They give grief. People come to the table for a lot of different reasons.

The Pharisees sat with Jesus and saw heaven come to earth. They saw a man who is God in flesh. They heard his remarkable teachings and watched him drive out a terrible disease with a mere touch. Right under their noses. They should not have been able to finish dessert as the same men they were.

But they couldn't get past one fact: Jesus healed on the wrong day—*God's* day, don't you know? Surely God would rather have the man suffer at least through sundown.[†]

Jesus asks another really irritating question, and you can almost hear the Pharisees' teeth grinding as he asks it. "What if you guys, you lovers of the law, have an ox of your own—or a child—fall into a well on the Sabbath? Just curious" (see v. 5).

---

†   I bet kids from the Pharisees' neighborhood knew their porch lights would be turned off on Halloween.

He knows the answer. They all bend the rules in that kind of situation. The leaders say nothing. But boy, if looks could kill.

Jesus would have seen this coming. Display the power and compassion of God, and he just knew they were going to get all self-righteous and condemny.

So he does one more filling. He fills their ears with a story, though I imagine he knows it's likely to slide right back out, with everything else he's said in their presence.

A Feast for the Least

Over this meal, Jesus wants to talk about a larger, very fine dinner. And later in the conversation, he does.

It's important to understand that in the Bible, a banquet is more than just a meal. It's often a metaphor for how God addresses the deepest needs of his people. Several of the parables involve banquets because the symbolism is so natural: the Master feeding his people, giving them not only food but *very fine* food—a simple and powerful image of God.

We have lots of banquets today, and great food is to be expected. But in the time of Jesus, eating a good, full meal was a huge event, even for relatively comfortable people. Jesus speaks often of feasts because it is such a vivid and enticing image for his listeners. They might think about the Passover meal, their ancient feast. As we hear this parable, we think of the Last Supper, and even the Marriage Supper of the Lamb in the book of Revelation.

God is the one who feeds us, who fills us. *Give us this day our daily bread.* It's basic. So Jesus tells the amazing story of the great banquet (found in Luke 14:16–24).

A man, he says, sends out invitations for a feast. When the table is set and the stove is hot, he sends a servant to say, "Dinner is served." But no one really wants to go. One of the invited guests says he has a field to inspect. A second has just bought some oxen, and he needs to work with them. "Sorry," says a third. "Just got hitched."

The host doesn't like hearing these excuses. As a matter of fact, he's offended. But he has all this delicious food, and the table looks so nice, so he sends the servant to go through town, to check the back alleys if necessary, and let the sick, the hungry, and anyone else know there's a nice meal waiting for them.

Mission accomplished, but there are still empty seats. The master *hates* empty seats. So he says, "Go out a few more miles—and hurry, this stuff is getting cold. Go down those country lanes. Check under the bushes if you have to. Let's get this party started."

And he makes a vow. Those of you who couldn't find the time—no soup for you!

Let's Meet the Cast

For the listeners, the best part of Jesus's parables is figuring out who is who. Some parables are very simple and universal; others, like this one, are pointed and filled with specific references to certain people.

God is usually identified as a king or a master of an estate or a business owner of some kind. Somebody definitely in power. But in this story, pay attention to the servant as well. Yes, he is Jesus.

God sent Jesus to invite us to the great banquet that is his kingdom, his life. As a matter of fact, in a similar parable in Matthew, the servant is murdered by the invitees, which makes the symbolism crystal clear. That was a prophecy as well as a parable.

The people invited to the banquet? Well, they're the people of God. But it turns out they're too busy to break away. You get the idea they're pleased with the invitation but otherwise occupied. They're actually polite, and it's easy to imagine many of them thinking, *Maybe I'll drop in later.* Just people in the rat race with the best of intentions but a few more laps to run.

Did you look at the excuses? Can you identify yourself in the story?

Business as Usual

The first guest has purchased a field, and he's eager to survey it.

Jesus is talking about personal gain here. Stuff. How often do we find people who believe they own property, only to finally realize it owns them? You run into them at the mall, months after they've disappeared from church or your Bible study group.

"We're just so consumed," they say, and somehow it sounds like they think that's a *good* thing. "Since we bought the house, we've needed to redecorate every room. We're going to come back, don't worry." It's as if God isn't as necessary now—house stuff will fill up their emptiness.

When I was watching a series of TV commercials recently, I started to notice that every commercial was selling something based on a presumption of emptiness. In other words, ad firms begin with the idea that you and I are missing something big from our lives. And they may be on to something. But in thirty seconds, they suggest that this car will fill the void—just look at the expression on that guy's face as he drives along a mountain road against a red sky.

That phone you bought last year? Outmoded. *This* one talks to you in a droning voice. You'll find yourself saying, "I honestly can't imagine how I ever got by without a phone that talks to me with a droning voice. Life is beautiful now."

The presumption of emptiness is the fuel that runs a consumer-based economy. In consumerism, we (of course) *buy* into the concept that our personal sense of fulfillment is directly related to our ever-increasing consumption of goods. A simpler way of saying it: if I feel a little down, I need to consume a little more. Late at night, when I lie in bed and feel emptiness, that's just life telling me that someone somewhere has this new thing that I don't yet have. Life is a cycle of ceaseless upgrading of inventory.

Have you ever watched a home video of a past Christmas or birthday? You're thrashing through the wrappers to all your presents, and on screen, it's clear you were delighted. But now you're noticing the *stuff* in the picture—did I ever actually wear that shirt? Whatever happened to that kitchen gadget? Gosh, I remember how much I wanted that jewelry, yet it's in the back of the jewelry box now.

Sooner or later, you wonder if you ever needed any of that stuff at all. But we're addicted. The Internet makes it possible to shop every day, even late at night, clicking on purchases we don't need and using money we don't have. Just browsing and salivating is a life. We hunt and we gather, and we can't stop for fear of what a moment of reflection might say.

I'm on an airplane right now, and an issue of *SkyMall* has been calling to me the whole time I've been writing this chapter. I'm going to take a break here and flip through it. See you in a few.

/

Okay, sorry. That was more than a few. It takes a while for me to make my way through a magazine when nearly every page features a product I didn't even know existed—and now can't seem to live without. I circled a few must-haves:

- **The Peaceful Progression Wakeup Clock**

  This is no ordinary alarm clock. According to *SkyMall*, "The clock gradually increases ambient light and stimulating aromas." It doesn't just make noise; it gets you up and going with quality scents and gradually increasing light!

- **Atari Arcade for the iPad**

  My favorite thing from childhood and my favorite thing from now, together for the first time. It's like 1985 and 2015 got married and had a baby.

- **A toilet seat that automatically lowers**

  I have no clue how it knows, but—it knows. Thirty seconds after your transaction is complete, it automatically shuts. Smart, considerate, and hygienic. I could make a case for this product winning a Nobel Peace Prize. Do you realize how many marriages it could save?

There's no end to the stuff that can be conceived. We go into debt to buy more and more of it. So why do we still feel empty? Your garage, your basement, and your storage unit may all be packed, and still you feel empty. It's a little like eating a big meal. You feel full at first, but it's not going to last. You'll always need the next meal, the next purchase, the next jolt of brief fullness.

We're trying to fill the cavity of the soul with things that won't fit. Mother Teresa said,

> The spiritual poverty of the Western world is much greater than the physical poverty of our people in Calcutta. You in the West have millions of people who suffer such terrible loneliness and emptiness.... These people are not hungry in the physical sense, but they are in another way. They know they need something more than money, yet they don't know what it is. What they are missing really is a living relationship with God.[1]

God's feast isn't just another square meal. No one's arguing that point. We believe it; count us in. We just can't stop consuming long enough to take our places at the table. And even if we did, we'd be looking at the dishes and decorations, wondering which store they came from.

Busyness Is Our Business

The second guest in the story talks about his new oxen. You might think he's simply another consumer. But the use of oxen tells us that this character is really concerned with work and responsibility and busyness. With five teams of oxen, he's going to get a lot more done, right? He can't wait to go plow the back forty, or eighty, or eight hundred.

In June 2012 the *New York Times* ran an article titled "The 'Busy' Trap" that caused a stir. It made the point that the default answer to "How are you doing?" is "Busy!" "*So* busy!" or "*Crazy* busy!" We roll our eyes and say it, pseudo-complaining, while in reality we're bragging. We establish our pecking order based on how little margin there is in our lives. The article then says,

> Busyness serves as a kind of hedge against emp-
> tiness; obviously your life cannot possibly be
> silly or trivial or meaningless if you are so busy,
> completely booked, in demand every hour of the
> day.... [We're] busy because of [our] own ambi-
> tion or drive or anxiety, because [we're] addicted
> to busyness and dread what [we] might have to
> face in its absence.[2]

There it is: busyness is a hedge against emptiness; it's a furious churning, driven by the vacuum inside us. We think we're running a business, but we may just be running. It's not all about the office either. Entertainment can fill up a lot of time; computers can become the closest relationships we have.

If you're an average American, you spend about one thousand hours a year watching TV.[3] So by the time you're sixty-five, you'll have watched TV for almost ten years of your life. Your ten-year-old self might be excited to hear that, but hearing it now sounds a little depressing, doesn't it?

There's worse news if you're in my generation or younger. It means you spend about five hours a day online via computer, phone, or tablet. In a lifetime, you'll therefore spend fourteen years connected to the Internet. Add on TV time and you've spent almost a quarter of a century staring at one screen or another.[†] It starts to sound like a prison sentence, doesn't it? But then, so does emptiness.

Let's talk about phones and busyness. The International Data Corporation (IDC) found that a whopping 80 percent of smart phone users check their phones within the first fifteen minutes of waking up. But some people check their phones all day, as if they have a nervous tic.

The *New York Times* is on the case with a think piece called "The Rise of the Toilet Texter."[4] Impressive title, by the way. The article claims that one in four Americans will not to go to the bathroom without their phones. That's a bold statement that raises serious questions. For example, what happens if the phone is dead and charging when they need to take care of business? When Mother Nature calls, she doesn't like being put on hold. And by the way, if you're talking to me during that time, I really don't want to know.

All this stuff is merely symptomatic of a calendar so jam-packed, a mind so distracted, and a life so oversaturated that when the time arrives for the great banquet, we can find no room for it.

[†] If you're reading this on a tablet, you're absolved. In fact, let's take the time you spend staring at a screen to read this book and credit that to your account. So play a few games of "Flappy Bird" on me.

The greatest tragedy is that people never know what they've missed. They're moving too fast and thinking too superficially, keeping up the pace, moving to the next item, busying themselves to places ever more distant from the God who loves them.

Like Sands through the Hourglass

The third guest to decline the banquet invitation might be the hardest to criticize—you want to slap him on the back and congratulate him instead.

"Hey," he says with a grin, "sounds like a nice dinner, but we're just back from our honeymoon. We have bags to unpack and thank-you notes to write, so we'll have to pass. You understand. We'll catch up with you at the next banquet."

The great drive of his life now is what sociologists call cocooning. The trend forecaster Faith Popcorn came up with this term in the 1990s, and it basically means, "I'm burned out on the social scene. This part of my life is about building a love nest, maybe a man cave, with a really great home theater. I just want to disappear into that place and enjoy my family."

How many songs about love have you listened to in your life? How many movies have you watched? Nearly all of them have a simple message: the right partner will fill the emptiness. By now it's ingrained in us. "You complete me." Happily ever after.

That idea causes people to marry and enter relationships with a huge and false expectation—that we'll be fulfilled by another human being for the rest of our lives. And think of the burden we're placing on that person. Romantic love is a gift of God, and it's one of the most wonderful he's given us. It's not the greatest gift, however. Only one relationship can fill us permanently.

Gary Thomas wrote a book called *The Sacred Search* that uses the word picture of marriage as an hourglass. He says the sands are moving through that hourglass, slowly but gradually. At first, the top area is full. We think our spouse is perfect. But the glass is turned over the moment we enter the relationship, and within twelve to eighteen months we begin to experience feelings of discontent. Emotions being what they are, the last grain of sand eventually hits the bottom.[5]

That's when we wonder what's wrong with the person we married—or with ourselves. Where'd the infatuation go? Where's the head-over-heels?

And … could there be someone else out there with a full hourglass, someone who could fill our empty spaces?

While we're grappling with these doubts, the idea of God flickers in our heads for a moment. It's as if someone is saying, "Come to the banquet. Just come."

And we think, *Not now. I have too many things to sort out. I'll catch up at the next banquet.*

Stuff. Activity. Romance. And there could be others. What would be your most likely reason for walking away? What takes up the space in your life that is meant for God?

Truly Filled

The great banquet is a metaphor, a word picture of the way God feeds and fills his children. He supplies our basic needs. But there is another kind of filling, one that is more immediate and direct.

As Jesus prepared to enter heaven, he told his followers of an event that would change them from the inside out. The Holy Spirit was going to come into their lives. Jesus said we would be *filled* with the Holy Spirit. When we become followers of Jesus Christ, he immediately enters our lives. We pray for his filling, which means a full cooperation with him and all he wants to do through us.

He is the presence of Christ with us, everywhere we go. He gives us special gifts for ministry. He counsels and comforts us, and each day he continues to transform us to the image of Christ himself—through tiny, almost imperceptible moments when we think something or do something that is the Jesus way, instead of our old way. And as we are filled with the Spirit, we begin to know what it means to have a truly full life.

In the book of Acts, the disciples change from the bumbling group in the Gospels to a dynamic, world-shaking band of godly revolutionaries. Filled now with the Holy Spirit, they are new people. Some have said that, instead of the Acts of the Apostles, the book should be called the Acts of the Holy Spirit.

Paul writes to the Ephesians, "Do not get drunk on wine.... Instead, be filled with the Spirit" (Eph. 5:18). Intoxication and spirituality seem like odd companions in a Bible verse. But Paul is saying it just right: don't try to get inspiration out of a bottle. God wants to fill and inspire you through his Spirit. If you need comfort, don't guzzle it. Find the real stuff in the one Jesus called the Comforter. Don't try to work up courage by drinking. The Spirit is courageous! The disciples ran in fright when Jesus was arrested, but they boldly faced danger every day once the Spirit had come.

Do you drink just to loosen up and relax? The fruit of the Spirit includes peace from God. Not to mention love, joy, patience, kindness, goodness, faithfulness, gentleness, and self-control.

An old commercial used to tout two merits of the beer it was promoting: "tastes great" and "less filling." At least the beer company got the second one right. Everything this world has to offer is less filling. And at the end of the day, none of it tastes great. But life in the Spirit is a different matter.

When Paul commands us to be filled with the Holy Spirit in Ephesians 5:18, he uses the present passive imperative tense. I know—ugh, grammar. But listen. The tense is imperative. It's not an option, but a command. It's not for certain denominations or just if you're into that kind of thing. *Be filled with the Spirit,* we're all told. *Do it.*

The verb tense also tells us it's not a one-time event. It's something we continue, just as we keep breathing and eating. As life chips away at you, be filled again with the Holy Spirit. Be refreshed.

The passive part of the tense means this is not something we do to ourselves. The jar doesn't fill itself, remember? Someone else must do that.

So how do we, the jars, place ourselves in the right position to receive that holy oil that never runs dry?

We empty ourselves. This we can do; we pray constantly to God, *Empty me, O Lord, of all the extraneous stuff, and fill me with your Spirit.*

The nineteenth-century evangelist D. L. Moody put it in these terms:

> I firmly believe that the moment our hearts are
> emptied of pride and selfishness and ambition

and self-seeking and everything that is contrary to God's law, the Holy [Spirit] will come and fill every corner of our hearts; but if we are full of pride and conceit and ambition and self-seeking and pleasure and the world, there is no room for the Spirit of God; and I believe many a man is praying to God to fill him when he is full already with something else. Before we pray that God will fill us, I believe we ought to pray that He would empty us. There must be an emptying before there can be a filling. And when the heart is turned upside-down and everything that is contrary to God is turned out, then the Spirit will come.[6]

Back at the great banquet, there's a moment of sadness. The servant is telling the master about the men who are simply too busy, too full to come and dine, no matter how rich and filling and wonderful the banquet.

But now the master smiles and says, "I like filling, so fill this table. Fill it with people who have room—in their schedules, their priorities, their souls. Fill it with *open* people. I don't care who they are, where they live, or what they've done. I don't care if they have the appropriate wardrobe or make sparkling dinnertime conversation. All I really want is emptiness."

Maybe you have that emptiness to give him. Or maybe you know Christ, but not closely enough. Let me repeat: the measure of filling we receive is in direct proportion to the level of our emptiness. Don't settle for the full life—go after the filled life.

Moody again: "God sends no one away empty except those who are full of themselves."[7] How sad it would be to starve to death just outside the door of the most delicious banquet in the universe, with the dinner invitation clutched in your hand.

Are you picking up on the aroma from behind those doors? Is your mouth watering yet? Come and take your seat and be filled.

Chapter 6

Helpless to Be Empowered

It stops now.

For too long, we guys have been the object of hurtful, insensitive stereotypes. These are promoted by those who are not guys (we won't name any genders). The cruel stereotypes revolve around guys not wanting to stop and ask directions.

Supposedly we will drive hundreds of miles in the wrong direction, while patient, all-knowing nonguys in the passenger seat implore us, "Please stop at the gas station and *ask* someone," "Will you do it just for *me?*" "We're *never* going to get there on time now," and, "Why do you have to be so stubborn?"

I know because I'm a victim of that stereotype. Until now. Because, before your very eyes, I will perform the research that blows up that myth for good. I have here an article on the subject from *American Psychologist.*[1] While I haven't read it yet, I have full confidence that there are enough guy psychologists out there to vindicate us.

Running my finger down the paragraphs and skipping the big words, I'm seeing there have been numerous studies done over three decades. Sounds good. And these studies now reveal (here it comes):

Men are less likely to stop and ask for help.

Okay, that's not what I was expecting. But as I continue to read, it does come out that:

Furthermore, men are less likely to go to the doctor.

When they do seek medical help, they ask fewer questions and share fewer symptoms.

Some of this helps to explain why men die seven years younger.

All right. Whatever. We guys do believe in self-reliance. We were taught by the guy-half of our parents to figure things out, to get things done, and not to throw like a girl. The study says we'd rather suffer than cough up the word *help*. But that's simply part of our masculine charm, don't you agree?

I have to admit the following. A couple of years ago, I planned a kayaking trip with my son Kael, who was eight at the time. Floyds Fork Creek runs behind our house, and we had decided to have an adventure. We'd explore the vast, uncharted wilderness of outer Louisville by water, then climb out somewhere and call my wife to come pick us up.

My wife thought it was a great plan except for one issue. "It's not a real plan at all," she said. Then she suggested we check Google

Earth and map out an actual, real-world bridge where she could plan in advance to meet us and pick us up.

I'm duly embarrassed by this, but her common-sense corrections only increased my masculine desire to do it my way. So I stood by my plan-which-wasn't-a-real-plan-at-all plan. As we continued to talk about the fun we were going to have, my oldest daughter and her friend said they wanted in. The trip was now close to qualifying as a party, so my youngest daughter joined the crew.

There were five of us. We borrowed kayaks from our neighbors and got into the water, and it was then that I realized I was responsible for four other lives. But I knew we'd handle it.

About forty-five minutes into the journey, the group was tiring out. I hadn't seen a single spot where we could climb out. At that point I decided to pull out my phone to check the GPS. The phone was protected in a high-tech piece of kayak gear known as a Ziploc bag, so I'd been proactive right there. Except the bag and the phone were gone.

Somewhere in the roaring rapids of Floyds Fork Creek, my phone had gone for a swim without my realizing it, which meant I couldn't check my GPS, which meant I had no clue where we were. And which further meant I couldn't call my wife to ask for help.

Two hours passed. Everyone was sweaty, soggy, and truly exhausted. My youngest daughter said, "This is not what I signed up for." Actually she said it quite a few times.

My eight-year-old son looked at me and said, "Dad, my arms aren't working right." Not good words for a father to hear. And things weren't getting any better. The sea was angry that day, my friends.[†] The sun was setting and it was getting dark.

At the three-hour mark, our trip qualified as an epic, placing us alongside other heroes of the open sea such as Jonah, Captain Ahab, and SpongeBob. At this point we finally spotted signs of civilization: a house with a backyard plunging down toward the sea—um, *creek*. A woman was doing some yard work. I was so relieved to see her, and I started to call out to her.

But I didn't. For some reason, the words, *Yoo-hoo, could you rescue us, ma'am?* just wouldn't form on my lips.

We began to pass the plunging backyard, and one of my daughters said, "Dad! Aren't you going to ask for help?"

What I said as I turned to my daughter was, "Hey, I'm sure there will be a bridge right around the corner." And the yard-work woman was still pulling weeds as she faded from view.

At Hour Four I was ready to surrender and repent. Darkness was closing in, both figuratively and literally. The kids were like zombies. This was the worst party my daughter had ever attended.

And there it was: a bridge. I whimpered a little as we made our way to the bank, and I was ready to ask for help from anything that had a pulse. Well, actually my plan was to send my son out to the road because almost anyone would want to help an adorable eight-year-old boy whose arms had stopped working. On the other hand, a frazzled man in his midthirties with wife-fearing desperation all over his face might scare away the rescuers.

† If you recognize that line, then you are always welcome around my table.

A car pulled over and rolled down its window for Kael, and I emerged from nearby trying to look casual, as if I were just catching up with my son. The driver handed me his cell phone so I could call my wife. It had been four hours since she'd dispatched us, *Deliverance*-style, into the precarious rapids of the neighborhood creek. She'd been expecting to hear from us within an hour, maybe an hour and a half.

She answered and, once she recognized my voice, said, "Let me guess. You lost your phone. You have no idea where you are. And I need to come pick you up."

Why didn't I take her advice in the first place? Why hadn't I asked the yard-work lady for help? Why did I send a boy to do a man's job by the roadside?

Because the good editors at *American Psychologist* know me too well. I am "less likely" to ask for help. If I can do anything in the world to tough things out on my own, no matter how unlikely, no matter how counterintuitive, I'll do it. Anything is better than getting to the end of me and admitting how much I need help.

Well, almost anything.

Poolside Helplessness

It's ingrained in our culture that we're supposed to take care of business on our own, without seeking assistance. Maybe that's why one of the most beloved of all Bible verses isn't actually in the Bible. Yes, it's this chestnut: "God helps those who help themselves." Just about everyone knows that one. People quote it, they love it, they try to live it, but it never crosses their mind that it can't be found in Scripture.

Maybe God forgot to put it in? I don't think so. A better explanation is that God actually helps those who *can't* help themselves. God helps those who stop in the midst of crisis and ask someone to assist them. When we're helpless and we know it, we're open to receive the transforming help he wants to give us. When we come to the end of ourselves, we find him there waiting to give us what we have been so desperate for all along.

John 5 tells one of the many biblical stories that prove that point. It's about a man who was crippled for thirty-eight years. Think about that—for nearly fourteen thousand days, he was incapable of walking, going where he wanted to go, or getting things he needed. That's a lengthy season of helplessness.

There might have been a time when he dreamed of a miracle. If he had been afflicted as a child, perhaps he would lie awake at night and think that tomorrow he would wake up to strong legs and a bright future. But morning after morning, the miracle never came.

Nearly forty years went by, and his spirit was hardened. He stopped praying and hoping. And he accepted the reality that he was helpless.

In this state of hopeless need, he encountered Jesus.

The man spent his days in a public place, lying on one of the five covered porches that surrounded the pool of Bethesda, located in the city of Jerusalem. For a great many years, skeptical scholars said this pool didn't exist. Some of them suggested that this meant the gospel was written many decades after its events and by someone who knew nothing about Jerusalem. But during the nineteenth century, the site of the pool was found, and it was just the way John described it.

The pool was associated with healing. You might find a footnote in your Bible telling you about the legend that an angel came down and stirred the water at certain times; afterward, the first person in would be cured.[†] That fact is written into later manuscripts of John, but not our oldest ones. At any rate, the Bethesda pool was a magnet for sick, blind, hurting, and helpless people. They came and watched for a change in the waters.

As a thirty-eight-year pool dweller, this man was a local institution. He had been there longer than anyone could remember. Most cities have colorful characters downtown who become part of the local personality. This man was like that. But you have to wonder about his motives at this point. Is he still struggling toward those waters whenever they stir? After all this time?

We picture him and think, sure, on some earlier day when he first came, he would have believed, *Today is my day. I'm going to be healed.* And he probably lived on happy thoughts and a few coins from passersby. But after enough years went by, his inner Joel Osteen must have fallen silent. He was all but rooted to the spot by now. He expected nothing but the coins that fell into his hands. Hopelessness was just part of the scenery for him.

Jesus sees the man and knows his story. That's what makes his question so upside down.

---

†   Think of it as high-stakes Marco Polo.

> One who was there had been an invalid for thirty-eight years. When Jesus saw him lying there and learned that he had been in this condition for a long time, he asked him, "Do you want to get well?" (John 5:5–6)

It's a strange thing to ask. A man is severely handicapped and spends all his days hanging out at a healing pool. Does he want to get well? Do people at the gym want to get in shape? Would Gilligan wish to disembark from the island?

Seems like a silly question—unless it's a loaded one. But the longer I serve people as a minister, the more I understand the question Jesus asks here. The answer is not self-evident at all. There are lots of people who like to hang around the waters without actually wishing to be healed. A lot of people come to church but don't really want God's help.

People do things for lots of reasons, not always the most obvious ones. They have motives they themselves may not even understand.

So Jesus gets right to the issue: You've been stuck in neutral for a while. Do you really want something better? Or have you laid down roots in a place of quiet desperation and low expectations?

Fear of Change

Who wouldn't want help? Someone afraid of change.

This man was sick for quite a duration. At a point approaching four decades, it was the only life he knew. He may not have liked it, but he had learned to survive as a beggar. Times were tough, but on the upside he hadn't had to learn a trade or put his back into hard work. His home was his mat. His community was the pool, and he was who he was. It's amazing what people can learn to endure.

And isn't there a touch of this man in all of us? We accept a lot of things that we know could be better. We say, "Well, that's just my life," as if it's engraved in stone. We decide God must want us to be here, because if he didn't, he'd make something else happen. In other words, we blame God. And if it's God's fault that we are in the situation we are in, then why would we ask him for help?

After a while we get used to things, and a limited life is less frightening than the thought of change. Resignation is better than disappointment.

I'd been on only a few dates with my future wife when I had to have knee surgery. It was nothing major—just a cluster of basketball injuries that needed fixing. Meanwhile, I wasn't sure what to think about this girl I'd been taking out. We'd had a few casual dates, and I couldn't tell whether she was really interested in me. She hadn't shown me much attention, and believe me, I was pulling out all the stops to get it.[†]

Knee surgery—a stroke of genius. Who knew? Once I was in recovery, she was offering that attention I had craved. Hobbling around on my crutches, with a brace on my leg, I was a pathetic figure—almost a shambling Precious Moments figurine, actually. I was the equivalent to George McFly in the movie *Back to the Future*, and it was working. Pity is highly underrated.[‡]

[†] She even seemed immune to my "Blue Steel" pose.

[‡] Single guys: Isn't it about time you got those plantar warts addressed? Just make them sound serious by using the scientific name, *verruca plantaris*. Or not. That sounds contagious.

Throughout my recovery, she started to do things that she had never done before. She sent me a passionately romantic card, which I still have. There's a picture of a frog on the front, and the caption reads, "Not feeling well?" Then, on the inside it reads, "Don't worry. You'll have your old bounce back in no time. Get well soon."

Okay, I guess "passionately romantic" is in the eye of the beholder. I read it my way, you read it yours.

She'd patiently walk with me between classes. And if we were in different places, she would check in to make sure I was all right. Then one day, as we sat together in chapel, she placed her hand on my knee brace.

I don't remember how long I was supposed to use the crutches and brace, but I remember thinking maybe I would use them a little bit longer, just to be sure. A month or so should do it.

To be honest, I wasn't sure I wanted to get my bounce back. I'd discovered there were things better than having my bounce. I was being showered with attention from a girl I liked. I was basking in the sympathy, and I liked not having to do anything but let someone else care for me. Did I want to get well? Not particularly.

I was trading her attention for something real. But I was afraid that once the crutches were gone, the attention would go with them. Fear of change can be highly motivating—and ultimately limiting.

Denial of Reality

Who wouldn't want help? Someone in denial of reality.

I imagine that after so many years, the man at the pool no longer had a healthy idea of what life could be if he stood and moved about town and took ownership of his life. Time did its thing, but so did environment. He spent every day and every night surrounded by hurting people. The world was compressed to the bounds of those five colonnades that defined the pool at Bethesda. He wasn't around too many healthy people, so unhealthy had become his new normal.

I watched a documentary about a thirty-four-year-old woman who had a three-hundred-pound tumor removed from her body. The tumor itself was twice the size of her initial body weight. It was a very horrific thing to see, needless to say. As the filmmakers documented this surgery, it was clear that they wondered why she had waited until the tumor was the size it was. All she could really say was that she didn't get help because she figured it would go away on its own.

The tumor was unique, but the attitude was not. We figure that our finances will sort themselves out in time. But the credit card debt keeps piling up, and still we keep spending. The tumor is growing.

We figure our teenage daughter will change her behavior and get with the program. Meanwhile, she's starting to cut herself. She's beginning to fall in with a very unhealthy group of kids, and she's moving further away from God by the day, but we decide to be patient. The tumor is growing.

We figure the problems in our marriage will fade away on their own if we don't address them. Who says we need help? Just ordinary husband-and-wife stuff, and it's nobody else's business. And within a few months, we're sleeping in separate rooms and he's feeling an attraction to someone at work. The tumor is growing.

Why not ask for help?

Ashamed of Our Condition

There are times when we approach the tipping point, we're tired of the anxiety, and we realize it's time to seek assistance. But we've waited a long time, and the situation has gone from bad to worse. Then we have second thoughts.

We step back and look at ourselves, and we feel ashamed. Asking for help requires an act of humility. We have to come as we are and present ourselves with our problems on full display. And we don't want some strange doctor involved with this thing. Or we don't want a marriage counselor umpiring this dispute. Or we don't want it to get out that we have issues with our daughter. If we talk to the pastor, if we talk to a family counselor, someone might gossip.

The woman with the tumor knew the tumor wasn't going any-where. It was more than clear that she needed help. But the size of it was embarrassing. Once she asked for help, there would be medical people staring at her like some kind of exhibit in a museum. There would be questions. There would be an end to hiding.

And the longer she waited, the worse the humiliation would be.

We feel deep shame, and the idea of public shame is unthinkable. We live under the tyranny of what other people think. Pride demands a terrible price. We'll actually suffer, as long as we think we can suffer quietly without others knowing.

As a pastor, I'm frequently asked to call a friend or a family member who is struggling spiritually. And I hear the story of a teenager struggling with addiction or a sibling who has decided not to believe in God. Maybe it's a husband who will no longer accompany his wife to church. "Would you talk to him?" I'm asked.

I once made those calls whenever asked, but today I rarely do. I've learned that it's unhelpful and maybe even counterproductive to offer help to people who haven't asked for it and won't admit they need it. Nothing is going to change until those people come to the end of themselves and willingly pick up the phone to ask for help.

That's why I tell folks, "Here's my number. Have them call me." Until someone wants to get well, there's not much that can be done.

I Think I Can't

Jesus asks the simplest kind of question—the kind that can be answered with yes or no. "Do you want to get well?"

The man's answer is none of the above.

> "Sir," the invalid replied, "I have no one to help me into the pool when the water is stirred. While I am trying to get in, someone else goes down ahead of me." (John 5:7)

Jesus has just been briefed on this situation, probably while the disabled man sat and listened. So when Jesus looks down and asks if he wants to be well, the man knows his motives are being called into question. And he launches into his well-worn excuse.

It boils down to *I can't.*

The book *Happiness Is a Choice* by Frank Minirth and Paul Meier is devoted to overcoming depression. In it, the authors discuss the tendency of Christians to say "I can't" when they find themselves confronted by obstacles. They write about how they cringe when patients use the words *I can't* and *I've tried,* which the two doctors identify as "lame excuses." Instead, they insist their patients use the words *I won't.*

When working with a man who says, "I just can't get along with my wife," the two counselors would make him rephrase that as, "I just *won't* get along with my wife." "I can't control my spending" would become, "I *won't* control my spending." They believe that the sooner people understand the place of their own free will, the sooner they can begin to move toward a cure.²

It's very true that people sometimes hide behind the words *I can't.* But we should add a qualification. We have to admit that there are occasions when people really and truly can't.

This is a book about coming to the end of ourselves, which is the beginning of the real adventure with Christ. We can make choices to align ourselves with that opportunity, but there are also realities that force us to say, "I'm at the end of my abilities. I've done what I can, but *I can't* live this life without Christ. *I can't* handle the problem of my own sin, and *I can't* rise and walk on my own.

Even then, we have to ask for help. The man by the pool could have done certain things. But in the end, only Jesus could help him, and it was a positive statement, not a negative one, to say to Jesus, "I can't. But you can."

The Hardest Thing

I met Lenny in the city of Colorado Springs.

I was on foot, walking to a restaurant near my hotel. A man approached me on the sidewalk and asked if I could spare just a few bucks. I checked my pockets, found a dollar bill folded into a wad, and handed it to him. "Thanks, man," he said.

As he was turning away, I stopped him. "Would you mind if I asked you a few questions?"

Lenny (as his name turned out to be) gave me one of those looks that you see on *Law & Order* when Ice-T is questioning a possible informant: "Yeah, but it's gonna cost you a little more."

I told him I had no more cash on me. But he thought about it and decided to cooperate anyway. He had no other place to go. So he submitted to a short interview.

"Where do you live?"

His eyes moved down the street, then back at me. "You're looking at it."

"Really? It can get cold in this town."

"I know a few shelters for the coldest nights."

"So how long have you been living on the street?"

"I'd say ..." He paused. "Eight years."

I thought about that and asked, "What's the hardest part for you?"

Lenny didn't hesitate. "Asking for help, man. Asking for help."

I was struck by that. No meal could be taken for granted. Weather was a constant threat. He had no real place for privacy—I could think of several hardships he faced. But for him, asking for help was the hardest obstacle of all.

Lenny and I talked a few more minutes, and he could see I was sincerely interested in his life. He talked about being homeless, and finally I asked, "If it's so hard for you to ask for help, what finally made you do it?"

He shrugged. "I had no other choice."

As I think about Lenny, I realize that when I finally come to a place of admitting I need help, I'm getting closer to the end of me.

The man by the side of the pool hasn't gotten there yet. Maybe a few chilly Colorado nights might have changed things. Maybe there were just too many people around, willing to let him keep living the same way. What he says, however, is that there is no one to help him. He's not saying he doesn't need help—clearly he does. He just doesn't have the helpers. How long ago did he stop asking?

Yet we have to admit, in the final analysis he's right. He can't walk, and therefore he can't get to the water. Not more quickly than others. While he may have stopped asking others for help, he at least acknowledges to Jesus that he needs help. He knows he can't make it to the pool on his own.

Jesus doesn't need to help him to the pool, of course. The living water has come to the man.

If the local legend that an angel comes to stir this water is really true, then the angel is certainly arbitrary. He's not much on reaching out in ministry—you can be several feet away for thirty-eight years, and it's too bad. You're out of luck.

That's not how it works for Jesus. In reality, he was always this man's only hope, just as he is ours. In a way, we're surprised that Jesus healed a man whose motives he questioned. He so often rewards pure faith with a healing. But here's the exciting point in this story. This man probably could have gotten some help. He could have managed to dip into that pool over the course of four decades. His story is more than a little sketchy. But Jesus doesn't shake his head and say, "You're not worthy." He heals a man who, even though he makes excuses, knows he is at the end of himself. Jesus comes to him. We're not asked to audition for the help of Jesus. All we need to bring him is our helplessness, and he meets us there at the end of ourselves.

We make the same mistakes this man made. We look for the pool. We go where the crowd goes and kind of hang out. We follow the ways of the world, and we tend to be disappointed when life never gets better. Jesus finds us, however, and he wants to change us once and for all.

The man does all that Jesus asks him to do. And right there, for the first time in thirty-eight years, he stands on his own feet, no longer helpless.

The boundaries of his world had been the five colonnades around the pool, but those borders rolled back to reach as far as the horizon. Now he can go almost anywhere, do almost anything. With the touch of Jesus, he is truly free.

Jesus addresses the man's helplessness in two ways. First, he heals the man through divine power. Second, he empowers the man to obey his command to stand up and walk.

Jesus says, "Get up! Pick up your mat and walk!" (John 5:8). That's three action verbs in one sentence—a life-changing moment for this man, and it's tied directly to a call to action from Jesus. Make no mistake, it is Jesus who does the healing. We don't participate in divine power—that's a one-way gift from heaven. But Jesus always gives us something to obey. He wants to move us from passive to active once again. So he comes to us and says, "Get up! Make your bed and move out. Life awaits you."

It's true for you and me too. Forgiveness for our sins is only the first part. He empowers us to stand and walk into a new life, to take on each new day in the power of the Holy Spirit.

We must come to the end of ourselves and be ready to listen and do what Jesus asks.

What Did the Phari-see?

This is a miracle story, so we expect the usual "happily ever after" ending. But actually it ends on a rather sour note.

The man stands on his own two feet. He feels exhilaration, wild joy. Just as Jesus asked, he picks up his mat to walk away. But wait! We find out in verses 9 and 10 that this is the Sabbath. Which, as we all know, means a Pharisee has to be lurking behind the bushes, waiting for someone to mess up and do a good deed.

Sure enough, religious leaders give the man a hard time. "You can't work on the Sabbath! The law doesn't allow you to carry that sleeping mat!"† (John 5:10 NLT).

Amazing, isn't it? These leaders knew the neighborhood and the man and his story. They just saw him miraculously cured, and all they can do is nitpick the fact that he lifted a mat on the day of rest.

Throughout the Gospels, they seem to give tongue-lashings to people who have just had wonderful things happen to them. It

---

† Hermeneutical exercise: go back and read that aloud in the high-pitched voice of a whiny six-year-old.

makes you wonder if their lives were so dry, so unfulfilling, that they couldn't bear to see joy and redemption in others.

I was in the car with my mom once when we spotted a bumper sticker that said, "Haters gonna hate." My mother isn't fluent in street language, so she asked for a translation. I could have pointed her to this verse in John. Haters gonna hate? Pharisees gonna Pharisee. They are rain clouds in search of parades. It's almost instinctive for any ordinary human being—flawed as we are—to see a wonderful moment of redemption and feel deeply moved. Most of us would have joined in this man's celebration. But the Pharisees wanted to make a citizen's arrest for unauthorized operation of a bedroll.

These days, if you send a Pharisee a YouTube video about a kitten being nursed back to life, he will criticize the cinematography.

A few months ago, a man gave his life to Christ at one of our church services. He happened to be wearing a baseball cap. At the end of the hour, a gentleman caught me in the hallway to let me know he was deeply concerned about the inappropriate headwear. Really? That was what he got out of that?

Here's your bumper sticker, sir.

Anyone who can be in a landscape of joy while maintaining immunity to it hasn't come to the end of himself. He hasn't experienced how good the good news really is. He should see that someone else's victory over hopelessness is our own victory, because Christ has brought the same liberation to every single one of us willing to say yes, to stand, and to walk. Once we've been to the end of ourselves and the beginning of Christ, we share our victories together, and parties break out at unpredictable moments.

God's Favorite Time

It doesn't matter if it's thirty-eight years, seventy-six years, or only thirty-eight seconds. God has no time limits. He has no limits at all. But he does have a favorite time, and that time is *now*.

Why not ask for help now?

Maybe because you hear the voices around you saying, "Not the time." "It's too late." "It's too embarrassing." "Just wait it out and work it out."

Maybe one of those voices is your own. You've drifted too far down the creek, and now you've given up and you're resigned to drifting some more. But there is no distance, no time limit, no reason at all. Jesus will come to you when you are at the end of yourself. He'll come when you're helpless and out of power. The man in John 5 learned that even thirty-eight years wasn't too late.

For two close friends of Jesus, Mary and Martha, death itself wasn't past the deadline. They expected Jesus to come to them, but Lazarus died before it happened. They were sure it was too late. But Jesus went to Lazarus anyway; he called his name and gave him a command very similar to what he told the man at the pool. "Lazarus, come out!" (John 11:43).

Jairus had a twelve-year-old daughter he adored, and she was dying. Jesus was heading that way when some of the servants came to say, "Don't bother. She passed away just a while ago." But Jesus told Jairus not to worry, but to have faith. In other words, *Don't stay down on the mat. Get up. Walk again.* And Jesus brought the daughter back, so that instead of a funeral, there was an amazing welcome-home party.

The disciples had fished all night and caught nothing. Empty nets meant an empty paycheck, an empty dinner plate. The disciples had to admit they were helpless. They were expert, master-class fishermen with nothing to show for hours of exhausting work. Then Jesus came to them and told them to cast their nets on the other side of the boat. Soon the nets were bursting. Jesus tells us, *Try it one more time—but this time in my power. It's never too late.*

As Jesus hung on the cross, a thief was a few feet away, also dying. There's no way to be more helpless than when there are nails through your wrists and ankles, your breathing is being cut off, and your life is ebbing away as people all around watch and shout curses at you. Jesus and a criminal, leaving this world together. Against all odds, the thief asked Jesus for help because somehow he understood it wasn't too late.

Jesus admitted him to heaven right there on the spot. The man had surely lived a terrible life, and in the last tiny fraction of a percentage of his life, one moment before his last breath, Jesus said, "I forgive you. Enter into the presence of the Father, to an eternal love and fullness you can't imagine. Get up from your cross. Rise from the dead and walk again. We'll go together."

All these people could have dismissed the invitation of Jesus when he came to them and told them to try it one more time. To get up. To have faith and be obedient. To rise from their mat, from their cave, from their cross, from their despair. Walk again.

It's not too late, and it never has been. And there's never been a better time, a more perfect time, than the present moment. That's always the one in which he wants to meet you.

The life you have is not the life you must accept. You need only to ask for help. The more helpless you are, the better—the more open you will be to the help that only he can offer. He meets you right there at the end of yourself.

Chapter 7

Disqualified to Be Chosen

Has this ever happened to you? A friend is showing you his home, and you walk by a piano. You ask, "Who plays this?" And your friend sits down and nails a Rachmaninoff rhapsody. When he asks if you play anything, you decide not to bring up the fact that you were quite the savant with the recorder[†] in the fourth and fifth grades.

Here's what you do the next time you feel like a talent-free lump. Are you ready? Go read some failed job applications. I found an archive of rejected ones online. I want to think these people were just having fun with the process. I really do want to think that.

For example, one applicant included a cover letter by his mother. Another was asked why he wanted the job and he said, "To keep my parole officer happy." Still another was required to list his achievements and boasted of graduating "in the top 85 percent of my class."[‡]

[†]   It's the small plastic clarinet deal from elementary school that grates on parents' nerves.

[‡]   For those of you who *weren't* in the top 85 percent, this person was saying, "I graduated in the bottom 15 percent." If anything else confuses you, just give me a shout.

There were lots of other impressive personal achievements listed. "Donated fourteen gallons of blood so far," shared one. Another insisted he is "fluent in multiple foreign … *accents.*"

How about qualifications? One lady made the point that "my twin sister has an accounting degree, so I know I'm good with numbers."

References? "Bill, Tom, and Eric." That's it.

Former employer? "Mom."

Sometimes the résumé is a little thin, so you might as well put a good face on it. It's tough knowing you're not qualified. With jobs, we know we need work experience, some level of education, and a good personal presentation.

Most of us would like to have the experience of serving God in some significant way. We probably even have some ideas about what that would be. Try completing this sentence:

More than anything I want God to use me to _____
_____.

I thought it would be interesting to try this on social media. So I put it out on Facebook and Twitter. Here are some of the replies I received:

More than anything else I want God to use me to:
- Introduce my family to Jesus.
- Show my cancer doctors the difference Jesus makes.
- Give God's love to the foster children in my town.

- Help addicts overcome their addiction.
- Rescue women who are trying to get out of adult entertainment.
- Save unwanted babies from abortion.
- Introduce my neighbor to Jesus.
- Use me as a single mom to raise my boys to be world changers.
- Start new churches in Eastern Europe.
- Share the gospel with prison inmates.
- Disciple my grandchildren.
- Rescue children from sex trafficking.
- Reach out to everyone in my neighborhood.
- Show my husband that Jesus has changed my life.

I wish I had the space to share all the great thoughts I got back. I recognize these as godly desires for service. But I was eager to ask each of these people, "So how are you doing with that?"

I imagine a number of them are moving forward. But others, I would guess, share their dreams with a certain regretful longing. They don't feel up to the task. They don't believe they're qualified. Where are you in all this?

You're eager to share that burden God has given you. Your hand is in the air, but God won't pick you—so you think. You could be unqualified because of what you're lacking, or maybe you feel disqualified by circumstances in your life. You look in the mirror and say, "God's going to choose someone else."

But what would he say? Let's take a look at how God has dealt with job applicants in the past.

The Long and Blinding Road

In this book we've listened carefully to Christ encounters—people crossing paths with Jesus in the Gospels. We've seen how he meets people at the end of themselves and gives them a new beginning.

The book of Acts has a famous and powerful story. It may be the most intense Jesus encounter in the New Testament, and it's not even in the Gospels.

The man's name was Saul, and he first appears in Acts 7. Up to this point, Acts has been dominated by Peter, John, and other disciples. But once Paul comes on the scene, he more or less owns the rest of the book. He then goes on to write much of the remaining New Testament. That encounter left a mark.

We receive only a glimpse of Saul before his one-on-one encounter with Jesus. Here a dynamic Christian named Stephen is carried out of town by a mob, and they stone him to death. "Meanwhile, the witnesses laid their coats at the feet of a young man named Saul" (v. 58). Just a cameo appearance, a face in the crowd.

Luke, the writer, makes sure it's clear which side Saul was on. He was in favor of the stoning. So we shouldn't be surprised by the next chapter. Time has passed, and Saul is now the mob leader. We're told he "began to destroy the church. Going from house to house, he dragged off both men and women and put them in prison" (8:3). He's not just anti-Christian in sentiment. Luke says he is *destroying* the church, home by home. He's an anti-Christian terrorist, uprooting a new faith before it can bloom.

Until Saul, no single individual had set out to wipe the Jesus movement from the face of the earth. He's the first archenemy of

Christianity. Then comes Acts 9. The language continues to be fiery: Saul is "breathing out murderous threats" against the Christians (v. 1). And, hearing that the Jesus movement is spreading into Damascus, a city in the north, he visits the high priest and asks for papers that will allow him to take his show on the road. He'll take a posse and bring back prisoners.

But as told in Acts 9:3–9, there is a turning-point moment—not just for Saul, but for world history itself.

Damascus is a six-day journey on foot. Saul is nearly there when suddenly a blinding light knocks him off his feet. *Literally* blinding. Someone calls his name and asks, "Why do you persecute me?"

"Who are you?" Saul asks.

"I am Jesus," says the voice, who then tells him to get up, go into town, and wait for instructions. Remember, Saul has that posse with him, and they've heard the voice too—but seen no one. But their leader is stone-blind. A proud and predatory man has to be helped into a city he has come to raid.

We might have expected God to knock this man down, sure—but then finish him off. Forgiveness? That would be surprising. But God goes well beyond that. He takes Saul and reinvents him as the leader of the Christian movement, the first evangelist to those outside the Jewish faith, and the first great theologian of Christianity.

If anyone was disqualified for leadership, shouldn't it have been a man who murdered believers and organized search-and-destroy missions against the church?

It's not that Jesus *needed* Paul. The movement was already winning converts and producing leaders. With a twist like this one, God was up to something. We have to conclude he was sending a message.

What was that message all about—and what does it mean for you and me?

"I Missed My Chance"

Sure, I admit Saul/Paul is kind of an exception to ordinary experience. It's like using Noah's ark as an illustration of a family vacation. Saul, who became Paul, was not just an everyday guy like you and me. He was a remarkable figure, before and after conversion—a born leader. Still, it's fair to ask what God was trying to say when he deliberately chose the least likely man on the face of the earth for the most important task on the face of the earth. What are the rules with qualifications and disqualifications anyway?

Apparently many people feel the standards are high and rigid. They'd love to serve, but they don't feel qualified. I challenge people to be Christlike presences in their marriages and with their children, in their neighborhoods and workplaces. There's a list of reasons people give for not stepping up, a common one being, "I missed my chance."

It's a time disqualification. The clock has run out. Reviewing the videotape of their past, people see where they could have done that great thing back then, but they missed their window of opportunity. Buzzer sounded; game over.

Chris Redman is a friend of mine who set records playing quarterback at the University of Louisville and then had a long NFL career. Recently I asked his thoughts on my going out for quarterback next season. In the NFL, of course. I like challenges.

Based on his immediate laugh, Chris clearly was not taking me seriously. I asked if he figured I couldn't take the beating.

"It's not that," he said.

"Good, because I can take it. I'm tough enough."

"No, you'd definitely take a beating. You'd take several on the first play. You'd break bones you never knew you had, but you'd heal. Physically."

"So what's the issue?"

"You'd be an emotional wreck for the rest of your life. Linebackers would visit you in your dreams. And when your son handed you the football, wanting to play catch, you'd turn and run out of the house shrieking."

I have to allow for the possibility that he could be right. I'm a late-thirties guy who missed his shot at the Super Bowl. I could have been a contender. It was clear even in the peewee league, where I showed my stuff.[†] Chris Redman has looked me over, and he says that ship has sailed. I'm pretty sure he also thinks that ship sank before it got out of the harbor.

My son is nine. We were watching the NFL playoffs together this past year, and I realized how differently the two of us see the game. For him it's one possible destiny. A Super Bowl could happen for him; he has a future. But I'm thinking, *Is this really only the second quarter? I'm ready for a nap.* He's leaning into a world of possibilities. I'm leaning back to grab another potato chip.

---

† "Son, every team needs a manager. It's an important job and you have what it takes." —Stan (my peewee football coach)

But what if that attitude carries over? What if we climb into the grandstand of life, disqualifying ourselves from getting into the game? What if:

- A marriage begins to sag, and she thinks, *Too late. We missed our chance.*

- Your children are making bad decisions and you want to step in, but you figure they won't listen. You've messed up parenting. They grew up before you could figure it all out.

- You see your neighbor seeking answers, and you know where they can be found. But you'd just get it wrong, you tell yourself. This happens only to the really cool people at church.

- You feel a little nudge to sit down and talk to your supervisor at work. You have some ideas about improving things. But you don't dare—who do you think you are, believing you could change anything?

You pull the milk carton out of the refrigerator and check the expiration date: "Best if used by January 7." Nothing's more useless than milk past its time. It smells nasty and tastes worse. In its time, it could have made a bowl of cereal happy. Just toss it.

How sad if some of us think God looks at us and sees an overdue expiration date.

"You Don't Want Me"

When I talk to people about serving God, one of the saddest responses I hear is, "God doesn't want me. Not after what I've done."

They assume God is just like a lot of people they know. He writes us off. He holds grudges. We'll never meet his standards. Our mistakes are many, our failures are well known, and our reputation is shot.

Don't you think Peter must have felt that way? Here's a guy Jesus personally chose and spent a lot of time with. It had to mean something when Jesus called him the Rock—what guy wouldn't like being given that name?

But after he did *exactly* what Jesus told him he would do, denying him at the moment of crisis, Peter retreated to his old life and figured he was off the list. Jesus had made it a point to tell him he'd fail. Why would he do that? Peter probably thought Jesus was saying, "You're not going to make it after all. Watch how you screw up in a few hours."

Peter went fishing, the only other life he knew. *That's it for me. My time came, and I struck out.* Out there on the boat that early morning, he reflected on the shipwreck of all his dreams. Jesus had qualified him, and that was a miracle. He had disqualified himself, and that was a tragedy.

Then he looked up to see a figure on the shore. Against all odds, it was Jesus, waving at him, telling him there was still work to do, and what was he doing out on that boat? *I still choose you.*

What about Moses? He had been raised like a prince, the world at his feet. But he lost his temper, killed a soldier, and fled into exile in the badlands of Egypt. From prince of Egypt to leader of the pack of sheep, just like that. Decades passed. He married and moved on. So did God, he figured. Then he saw something bright—a bush in flames, and with it a voice, commissioning him. *I still choose you.*

Matthew sat at the tax collection booth. He had betrayed his own people to collaborate with the Romans. He traded his self-respect and good name for a few pieces of gold, and it was a bad deal. He knew that now. He couldn't buy out of his loneliness.

Then the Teacher, the Healer, walked by and said, "Follow me." *Just the same, I choose you.*

I'm sure every one of these people was surrounded by jabbering voices all too ready to bring up the past. "What were you thinking, Peter?" "You're a has-been, Moses!" "You did it to yourself, Matthew!" People love reminding others of their plight. Perhaps they feel better about their own failures if they can make others feel bad about theirs. They keep score, and they give more updates than ESPN.

It's going to happen. The problem is that we listen to them. We take them to heart.

Sometimes my record gets me in trouble around the house. Maybe other husbands grapple with this one. Let's just say you didn't do it. Sometimes the dog really *does* eat the homework—why is that so hard to accept? At any rate, your reasonable explanations are discarded. You are guilty until proven innocent.

Maybe (just for the sake of argument, okay?) you come home from work and your wife wants to know where you hid the TV remote. It's a loaded question, right? She assumes facts not in evidence. *Anyone* could have snuck into your house and hid the remote. Has she done DNA testing? Interviewed witnesses?

But in this totally random example, you know for a fact you did *not* hide the remote control, mainly because you have not *used* the remote control within recent memory. But because of your past guilt and subsequent conviction, instead of taking a stand for a fair trial, you listen to your inner I'm-not-good-enough megaphone. Before you know it, you're convinced you're a bad husband. An ineffective family leader, resigned to being a silent breadwinner with remote-control restrictions. You're paralyzed, totally stopped, even though you're sure the real remote hider could be out stealing other electronic accessories right now.

Coming to the end of me also means allowing Jesus to put an end to the guilt and shame of the past. He deletes your permanent record and offers you a new beginning with a new purpose.

"They Won't Forget"

We have a hard time letting people off the hook sometimes. As hard as it is to forgive, it's even harder to forget. Through Christ, God refuses to look at our past. That's all been handled, set right, and paid for. God wants us to forget what is behind and move toward what is ahead. But that's God. It's not as easy for us mere mortals, even though we're called to live by the same policy.

For those of us worried about how others see us, we have to move forward even if we don't know where we stand with them. God determines your future, not others. If he says go, then go. It could be that you'll disprove the doubters and teach them something about God's grace.

Paul came from a culture where memories went back one thousand years. His people remembered everything about their history, their heroes, and definitely their enemies. No culture anywhere placed more stock in the past. They also recalled what Paul had been up to recently. Can you imagine their first impression when he turned up with a big smile, saying he'd joined the club?

I imagine he had a pew all to himself. This guy was an executioner with blood still drying on his hands. There was something else too—how was he even qualified, when so many of the believers had actually known Jesus, helped to build this young church, and taken time to digest the Master's teachings?

In Acts 9 we find Paul still sitting quietly in Damascus, blind and most assuredly confused. Life has no sharper left turns than the swerve he had just taken. At this point, the Lord calls on a man named Ananias, a local church member, to go see Paul and lay hands on him. Now, it's true that a lot of Christians would have liked to lay hands on the old Saul. He had definitely laid hands on plenty of them. So it's not surprising to read the reaction of Ananias.

> "Lord," Ananias answered, "I have heard many reports about this man and all the harm he has done to your holy people in Jerusalem. And he has come here with authority from the chief priests to arrest all who call on your name." (vv. 13–14)

God replies in the next verse, "Go! This man is my chosen instrument to proclaim my name to the Gentiles and their kings and to the people of Israel."

Ananias was human. He couldn't help but take the past into account. But God asked for faith and obedience. His plan and his will are all that matter, because the lesson he's teaching almost always flips our assumptions on their head.

I officiate at funerals, occasionally for someone with a BC and an AD in his or her life—for example, he lived one way, then Christ changed him. At the funeral, there will be guests who knew this person only from the old days. So I hear BC stories, as well as AD stories.

Frank passed away in his midfifties from a heart attack. He was a strong believer who loved his family and lived each day for Christ. His family wanted a time in the service for people to share a few words or a favorite story.

From a human perspective, I love those moments. From a planning perspective, I sit on pins and needles. You have no idea what someone might step up and say.

In this case, a few of Frank's college buddies came up to the microphone together and shared some stories about how they'd enjoyed getting drunk with Frank and how much he'd loved the party life. One of them said, "He was picky about his cars, but not his girls." Needless to say, they hadn't seen Frank in years. The old friends continued to share details that I knew must be painful to the family.

My plan was to walk up and say a few words about the difference Christ makes, how the past is washed away. But Frank's brother-in-law got to the microphone first. He said, "We all know Frank died a few days ago. But the Frank that you guys described died many years ago."

Many people would disqualify themselves for serving God because of their past. Not Paul, though, and thankfully, not Frank. How about you?

"I Dishonored My Good Name"

For this very reason, God often renamed people—Simon became Peter; Jacob became Israel; Saul became Paul. These were new men with brand-new lives. Because of Jesus, Saul was forgiven, his crimes pardoned, and he was free to become Paul, a radically different man. His résumé was null and void, and the only qualification that mattered was that God said, "I choose you."

What's the past burden you're still carrying? Adultery? Go talk to David the king. Lying? Deception? Abraham and Isaac knew a little about that. A sordid past? God chose Rahab, a prostitute. Anger and temper issues? James and John fit into God's plan anyhow. Have you ever dropped the ball at the worst time? John Mark did too. How about a string of bad relationship choices? The woman at the well knew what that was like, and God sent Jesus with a message just for her.

Maybe today it's your turn. Jesus has a message for you. It has nothing to do with your qualifications. It has to do with coming to the end of yourself, because that's when God can use you in the very best way. By his grace, and by nothing you can offer, *he chooses you.*

In fact, you may feel held back by one particular issue, and that issue is precisely what God wants to use. It's actually one of God's favorite strategies. Your "disqualifier" becomes God's qualifier. From what you've seen of the teachings of Jesus, how else would you expect him to do things?

Chuck Colson understood that. His whole life had been built on prominence, achievement, and building a reputable name. He served presidents. He moved in the highest circles of power. But after going to prison in the wake of the Watergate scandal, he figured he was done. The central qualifications of his life had been shredded. His "good name" was a subject of jokes on late-night talk shows. But when he came to the end of himself, God was just getting started. Here's how Colson described it:

> The great paradox [of my life] is that every time I walk into a prison and see the faces of men or women who have been transformed by the power of the living God, I realize that the thing God has chosen to use in my life ... is none of the successes, achievements, degrees, awards, honors, or cases I won before the Supreme Court. That's not what God's using in my life. What God is using in my life to touch the lives of literally thousands of other people is the fact that I was a convict and went to prison. That was my great defeat, the only thing in my life I didn't succeed in.[1]

In 1 Corinthians 1:18, Paul wrote that the message of the gospel is foolishness to the rest of the world, but followers of Christ recognize it as the power of God. In other words, our entire faith is built on God being glorified through what looks to everyone else as failure and defeat.

Paul was speaking of the cross, a symbol of utter shame and humiliation at that time. The Romans put thieves and killers on crosses. The Christians then used the cross as a symbol of God's power. Why would anyone do that? Because it's wisdom. Because everything we knew was wrong.

The end of me, the gutter and grave of my life experience, is where I encounter the power and redemption of God, who is glorified through Colson's prison term, John Newton's slave trading, and Saul the hunter, who tried to destroy the church and then spearheaded its expansion throughout the known world.

What's your point of disqualification? How is God going to use it?

"I'm Not Ready"

You hear all these things and nod your head. Sure, it's all true. No way to argue with the biblical account and God's track record after that—he can use anybody, even you. But you have one last excuse card to play: "I'm not ready."

It's one of the classic get-out-of-jail-free cards. You say, "I need to learn more first. I need to grow more. I want to be at my very best. I don't want to jump into anything before I've done all my homework."

It sounds downright prudent and sensible, doesn't it? Over the years, I've seen people with kingdom success written all over them. I knew it was only a matter of time before God did something extraordinary through them. I watched them over time as they got ready,

got ready—then got ready some more. They never seemed to gradu-
ate from the school of getting ready. One more Bible study group. A
little more time praying for God's will. It's a little like the guy who
keeps walking out on the high dive, looking down, and saying, "I
need to work a little more on my form."

Just jump! Jump *before you're ready to jump.*

Paul is baptized. His eyesight comes back, but his bloodlust
doesn't. Everything in his life has been turned inside out. He spends
a few days with the disciples in Damascus. Then he begins to preach
Jesus in the synagogues (see Acts 9:20). This is a few days after coming into town with a letter from the high priest allowing him to find
and arrest Christians. And now he's *preaching?* What, he went to the
weekend seminary?

Paul had a process like everyone else. He was on his way to growing and learning for the rest of his life. Discipleship is a discipline,
and it's not to be minimized. But God told him to get started, and
he said yes.

The most effective Christians—the ones most likely to tell their
friends about Jesus—are often newly reborn believers still filled with
fresh excitement. It's also true that the longer people are in the fold,
the more likely they are to figure out that others have more information and that maybe they themselves aren't "ready" after all.

Paul didn't have all the information yet. He hadn't even made
it home or told any of his friends what was up. But he was hearing
from God now, in a way he never had in the past. The Holy Spirit
was filling him and saying *go.*

Somewhere inside, there was probably another voice that said,
Not yet! Take some time with this thing. But listen to what Paul told us

later: "For the Spirit God gave us does not make us timid, but gives us power, love and self-discipline" (2 Tim. 1:7).

You might feel a bit of eagerness or nervousness. God doesn't deal in jittery nerves. Boldness comes from the Holy Spirit. He doesn't take account of our lack or our what-ifs. Don't have the courage? He'll give it to you. Don't have the words? He's got you covered.

In what seems like the smallest of moments, in brief encounters with other people, he'll take you and speak a life-changing word through you. When God chooses you, he equips you. Every time.

Let me leave you with one of those brief encounters.

Enter Mission

I was at a play with my wife. I'm not much of a theater junkie, to tell the truth. I worry some guy in tights might suddenly break into song. But I love my wife, and this was an anniversary date.

We made it to halftime. Sorry, intermission—that's what they call it, right? I'd been a little restless, but now the lights came on and I looked around. The guy next to me smiled and we struck up a conversation. He was a lawyer and was accompanied by his daughter, who had just graduated from high school. "That's great," I said. "We have three daughters at home."

He glanced over at his daughter and told me, "Seems like just the other day she was a little girl. I wasn't much of a father then. Short temper, busy schedule. You know." He looked at me a little closer and said, "Mind if I tell you something else? Something that happened to me when she was six and changed me for good as a father?"

"Of course not. Go ahead." I laughed and said, "I can use all the dad-and-daughter advice I can get."

"Well, for six years I was a lousy husband and father, but I was climbing the ladder quickly on the job. That's what mattered most to me, you know? I can see now, though, what I couldn't see then, that my home was falling apart."

"What happened then?" I figured I was going to hear about a health scare or his company crashing. This was much more compelling than the play.

"A friend of mine invited me to church." He quickly added, "Now, you'll probably say you don't care much about organized religion, but listen, I didn't either."

It was about this time I realized this man was about to witness to me. I'd encountered an annoying street preacher or two, but other than that, no stranger had ever talked to me about Jesus.

"I had no intention of going to church at first," he said. "But this friend just kept pestering me until I gave in, just to get him off my back. And this may sound a little weird to you, but I met Jesus there at church. It changed everything for me. It's the best thing I ever did."

I wanted to get in a word here somewhere and clue him in that I was a preacher, but he was on a roll. "Hey, you don't know me from Adam, but you have daughters and I thought I'd tell you what changed things between me and my own."

That daughter had been listening to our conversation, and she leaned across him now and gave me a wonderful smile that seemed to say, "My dad is the greatest."

Then intermission was over. The lights went back out, and that was fine with me because my eyes were welling up with tears. A man I didn't know—an attorney, a husband, a father—had told me how Jesus changed his life. And he did it by laying out his disqualifications, showing me all the reasons he should have failed.

That's how the power of God shows through. He loves to take our messes and make them his masterworks. How else can you explain a heart utterly transformed, except through the love and grace of Christ? What is the source of that daughter's wonderful smile, when the family once teetered on the edge of catastrophe?

The biggest reason you can't get it done is the precise reason he can—maybe the precise setting he wants to use. What is it for you? A limitation? A memory? An age? A fear? Doesn't matter. File away your disqualifications. Surrender them. Renounce them (over and over again if you have to). Get to the end of yourself and you'll find you are in the right place to be used significantly by God.

Chapter 8

Weak to Be Strong

I had agreed to speak at a seminary for a conference with the theme of "The Leadership of Jesus." I wasn't sure what aspect of Jesus's leadership they wanted me to focus on during my session, but I liked the idea and figured I could adapt my talk to the specific session when I arrived.

The time grew near, and I received a little more information. Uh-oh. I was speaking late on a Saturday morning. I'm not sure how I had missed that detail, but it was going to be an issue. The church where I preach has a Saturday afternoon service, and I couldn't speak at the seminary and drive back in time to preach at church. Flying wouldn't work either—airport time, and all that. Backing out of a commitment was something I absolutely hate to do, but it looked like the only option here.

Then I had the brainstorm.

A member of our church flies helicopters as a hobby. And I'd always had a hankering to take a copter ride. Here was the perfect chance to kill two birds with one stone. He could fly me to the conference, where I would step off the whirlybird and do my thing. Then he'd fly me back to church. He told me he was happy to help, and it seemed that everything was going to work out.

I met him on a cold Saturday morning, and we lifted off into the wild blue yonder. I was having a blast, and not just because copters are cool. It's a little embarrassing to admit (actually this is really embarrassing), but I felt pretty important and prestigious choppering in to speak. At least subconsciously, I must have been figuring the attendees were going to say, "Wow. Who's that guy?"

It was a snowy weekend, and the hosts had cleared the snow away so the helicopter could land right beside the chapel where I'd be speaking. I did wonder how distracting it would be for the speaker of that moment—all that "whoop-whoop-whoop" of the whirling blades, people holding down their hair, small animals being carried by the gusts. But hey, it goes with the territory for the copter crowd. What could I do? High-powered figures must deal with such dilemmas.[†]

As we landed, I imagined all the heads craning to see the "bird," wondering why there was a *Black Hawk Down* reenactment at their Bible conference. Was the president of the United States about to step off of it? No, just me, but I saw myself strutting in slow motion as I tossed off a cool salute to my pilot.

I stepped inside with about fifteen minutes to spare before my session. An aide walked over and handed me a sheet of paper

---

† Please tell me you know me well enough by now to recognize my use of sarcasm. If I seem to be expressing the opposite of the chapter theme, this generally means I'm being facetious. If you didn't pick up on that, my writing may be rough going for you. Sorry about that (sarcasm again, right there). If you're still not getting it, I look forward to your comments on the Internet (yep, still sarcasm).

with the precise title of my talk. My cheeks flushed as I read it: "Leading from a Place of Weakness."

Duh! *Well played, Lord. Well played.*

I had arrived with some serious swagger, some extra-strength pomposity, making the gaudiest entrance imaginable, only to speak on humble servant leadership. No cute escapes for this one. It would be dishonest to claim it as a stunt to illustrate my theme, although the thought crossed my mind.

No, I had to own it. My seminar began with a time of confession and acknowledgement of how much I still needed to learn about the subject I was getting ready to teach on.

Jesus gets us like that frequently, if we're paying any real attention. We tend to revert to the human default, which is pride and self-importance and the deep desire to impress others. Getting to the end of me means coming to the end of my strength. As we will discover in this chapter, our weaknesses create a space that God wants to fill with strength.

In through the Servants' Entrance

Weakness.

It's a pretty big deal to Jesus. Even his birth was a carefully constructed teaching moment. He didn't step off a helicopter, waving at the movers and shakers. We've looked at so many manger-scene Christmas cards that we've built up an immunity to the point here: he came in appalling weakness—by way of a poor teenage girl with almost nothing going for her. Mary and Joseph couldn't even pay for a sacrificial lamb at their child's birth, as required by Levitical law. They had to choose the cheap alternative, offering two birds.

Irony? The parents of the Sacrificial Lamb of the world couldn't offer an *ordinary* sacrificial lamb. The Prince checked in as a pauper and proceeded to grow up on ten acres of nothing called Nazareth.

We love the image of a serene, sweet manger scene, but let's face it. This was a feeding trough for livestock. It was the smelliest delivery room imaginable. Sometimes I think of this at Christmas when my wife pulls out the scented candles. It's her "Fragrance of the Season" collection, with Apple Pie, Cinnamon Spice, and even one marked "Nativity-Scented." It's fair to say that description isn't accurate, because the aroma of fresh cow flop doesn't quite come through.

Have you seen "mandles"? Yep, scented candles for men. "Auto Shop." "Bass Fishing." And my favorite, "Slab of Bacon." Why don't women try to attract their man with that perfume?

True "nativity scent" candles need to be more along those lines. "Shepherd Sweat." "Dirty Donkey." "Camel Dookey."

We sing, "The cattle are lowing" without thinking about how upside down that really is. Why poverty? Why a stable? Why blue-collar shepherds?

Because he's God, and God chooses weakness as the best setting to display his strength. Weakness creates the space that God fills with his strength. Do you think it all happened by chance—that God entered history in flesh at that moment, as planned before the foundation of time, without doing his research? Forgot to make reservations at the inn for his Son?

Hardly. An artist knows how to make something "pop," as they say on interior decorating shows on TV.† You set something off by putting it in a setting where it can't be missed because it's framed to its best advantage. And God is the artist of all creation. On a field of pure weakness, poverty, and obscurity, power and royalty pop.

He could have disembarked in one of the world's great cities. People would have said, "Right time, right place. Look what fate can do."

He could have been born into a billionaire financial dynasty. People would have said, "Look what money can do."

He could have been the child of an earthly emperor. People would have said, "Look what political power can do."

He could have come by way of a celebrity family. People would have said, "Look what fame can do."

Instead, he stepped into poverty, weakness, and obscurity, and all we're left to say is, "Look what God can do." He takes a blank canvas of drab gray and says, "Watch this!"

Coming on Strong

The idea of weakness being something to celebrate isn't just counterintuitive; it's countercultural. In our world strength is valued—not weakness. That was true in the first-century world as well. When Paul wrote to the church in Corinth, he knew the idea of celebrating weakness would be difficult to swallow.

† Or so I'm told that's what they say on decorating shows. I have no way of personally knowing that.

Corinth was known for lavish lifestyle, impressive skyline, and socialites who loved the nightlife and liked to boogie. It was a setting of strength and accomplishment, a place our culture would recognize—emphasizing success, self-reliance, self-indulgence. "Self-everything," unfortunately. Once we live that way, we cut ourselves off from the things only God can offer.

Paul had learned the hard way that weakness is the entry point for experiencing the strength of God. Now he wants to communicate that to the Corinthians, but he knows in order to get a fair hearing he will need to speak to them from a place of strength. So Paul decides to dig up the résumé he used to clutch so proudly, blow off the dust, and use it to show he can meet the jet-set Corinthians on even terms. Then he won't sound like a weak guy selling weakness.

As he starts to talk strength, he keeps admitting how silly he feels doing it:

> Whatever anyone else dares to boast about—I am speaking as a fool—I also dare to boast about. Are they Hebrews? So am I. Are they Israelites? So am I. Are they Abraham's descendants? So am I. Are they servants of Christ? (I am out of my mind to talk like this.) (2 Cor. 11:21–23)

It's as if he's having a hard time keeping a straight face. As if he offers his street cred for the sake of argument, but he wants it understood it's something he left far behind. As if he'd just seen a sunrise at the Grand Canyon and someone asked him to share the finger painting he did when he was seven.

In the next chapter, Paul grudgingly continues on with his spiritual credentials, and he drops a bomb.

> This boasting will do no good, but I must go on. I will reluctantly tell about visions and revelations from the Lord. I was caught up to the third heaven fourteen years ago. Whether I was in my body or out of my body, I don't know—only God knows. Yes, only God knows whether I was in my body or outside my body. But I do know that I was caught up to paradise and heard things so astounding that they cannot be expressed in words, things no human is allowed to tell. That experience is worth boasting about, but I'm not going to do it. I will boast only about my weaknesses. (2 Cor. 12:1–5 NLT)

Imagine them reading his letter aloud to the church, and when they get to this part someone says, "Wait. What?" An old guy taps at his hearing aid. A couple of others peek over the reader's shoulder. Did he just say he was caught up to the third heaven?

And this thing went down fourteen years ago? Seems like he might have mentioned it before now. Even now, he just drops it in, kind of half-apologetically. He hates to bring it up, but, you know, he visited Heaven #3, so there's that.

Me, I thought I was important because of a helicopter ride. If I were Paul, I can tell you I wouldn't make it fourteen years without telling my friends about dropping in on angel turf. I'd be on Instagram in fourteen seconds.

> Hey, visited 3rd heaven today. #nofilter
> #whatdidyoudotoday

I would work it into every conversation. It wouldn't matter what the subject was at the time. People could be discussing politics or football and I'd say, "Well, you know, when I was caught up in the third heaven—I did mention that I was caught up in the third heaven, right?"

I wouldn't be writing this book. I'd be writing one called *The Third Heaven: Thoughts on Why God Chose Me and Not You.* The movie would be called *Third Heaven Is for Real.*

I would immediately update my bio: "When not being caught up in the third heaven, Kyle enjoys spending time with his family."

Yet Paul didn't see fit to mention it for a decade and a half. His bio read this way: "A slave of Christ."

Slavery was no impressive credential to anybody at all. The only talking point was the identity of his or her master.

Paul is saying in this section of his letter, "Sure, I've got the background and the Hebrew heritage. I've paid my dues—I've been shipwrecked, beaten, stoned, imprisoned; I've been cold and hungry and all but martyred, and you want spectacle? I've tripped the light fantastic, gone on a supernatural journey. So if I'm trying to be the alpha dog of the first-century Christian lecture circuit, I could probably put on a little cockiness, no problem. But let me tell you why that's not happening."

A Thorny Problem

Paul then drops another bomb, one more tantalizing to modern readers because he refuses to put a fine point on it.

> So to keep me from becoming proud, I was given a thorn in my flesh, a messenger from Satan to torment me and keep me from becoming proud. Three different times I begged the Lord to take it away. (2 Cor. 12:7–8 NLT)

How do you stay grounded after being caught up to the third heaven? You struggle. You deal with some kind of physical problem you can't shake. You can't have your head in the clouds when you live with a backdrop of significant pain.

As you can imagine, there's been a twentieth-century guessing game about what the "thorn in the flesh" was. Whatever ails him, he seems to feel it's between himself and God. For our purposes, we know a thorn is not a splinter; the original word choice could be translated as *spear* or *stake*, so this is a bit more than a pesky cold or a nasty paper cut. He suffered enough that he didn't *ask* God to remove it—he begged.

Paul was a hard-driving overachiever, and this thing was slowing him down. He wanted to pray, *Lord, think how much more I could do for you if you took the pain away.*

But perhaps the still, small voice replied, *It's not about what you can do. It's not your strength that is necessary.*

Paul continued:

> Each time he said, "My grace is all you need. My power works best in weakness." So now I am glad to boast about my weaknesses, so that the power of Christ can work through me. That's why I take pleasure in my weaknesses, and in the insults, hardships, persecutions, and troubles that I suffer for Christ. For when I am weak, then I am strong." (2 Cor. 12:9–10 NLT)

That last sentence is the payoff—the wisdom God taught him. God is always strong, but in our weakness that strength goes viral. The world sees that it's not about anything but him. At the end of me, I find a strength in God that I never would have experienced otherwise.

This is so difficult for us, in part because we're facing a lifetime of cultural programming. From childhood, we're taught that strong is good—as of course it is. We want to be strong and healthy. We want to have a strong education and strong values. What Paul is talking about is the difference between *having* strength and *leaning on* it. The world says to grow strong, be strong, and depend on your strength. God says to grow strong but to know that his strength is what really counts. So lean on that.

We're taught to believe, "I can do anything I set my mind to." The gospel says, "I can do all things through Christ."

We're taught, "Never let them see you cry." The gospel says, "Know that in your weaknesses, Christ shines."

As I've thought and studied over the years, I've changed my mind in some ways. Once I would have made the case that God works *despite* our weaknesses. Or God works *around* our weaknesses. But that's not a strong enough statement. It's not the real point. God doesn't demonstrate his strength *even though* we're weak—he demonstrates it precisely *through* the weakness.

Otherwise we wouldn't even matter in the issue of God's power and glory. We'd just need to get out of the way and let him do his thing. But this life is a dialogue, a relationship between God and the children he loves. Like the adoring parent he is, he wants us to be a part of everything he does. Does he really need you or me to do anything at all? No; he *wants* us to work with him because it pleases him and because it's more meaningful to those watching.

Look at the disciples Jesus chose. Did he hold auditions and interviews, looking for the most articulate, most talented, most influential and persuasive? That's how they gather those special-mission teams in movies. "This is Bud; he's a master of disguise. This is Charlene; she's a demolitions expert. This is Carlos; he can hack into computers."

Jesus saw some fishermen and a few others and asked them to follow him. That was it. As a matter of fact, it turned out to be their weaknesses—so painfully obvious during the ministry of Jesus— that made their testimony so powerful. After Jesus ascended, Peter and John spoke to some religious leaders.

When they saw the courage of Peter and John
and realized that they were unschooled, ordinary

men, they were astonished and they took note
that these men had been with Jesus. (Acts 4:13)

God was glorified, not *despite* their lack of education or talent, but *because of* it. These were ordinary, unimportant men. When they did spectacular things, people had to give another thought to what had happened to make them who they were. It was their weakness that made space for God's power to be demonstrated.

Corrie ten Boom is best known as the author of *The Hiding Place*, an account of her time as a prisoner in a German concentration camp and as a witness for Jesus. She wrote another book, less well known, titled *Tramp for the Lord,* in which she told about a woman she met in Russia during the Cold War, when Christians were being persecuted.

The old woman, Corrie wrote, was reclining on a sofa. Multiple sclerosis had done quite a job on this woman. Her body was twisted in every direction, and she depended on pillows to prop her up. She had no mobility, so her husband's time was consumed by her care. The index finger of her right hand was all she could control. Nothing else.

But oh, what she got from that finger. It moved across a typewriter keyboard all day and late into the night, tapping out words and sentences and paragraphs as she translated the Bible and other Christian books into her Russian language.

Her husband watched and noticed that it often took the wrinkled old finger quite a long time to hit a key—but on it moved, letter by letter, through books of the Bible.

And then Corrie ten Boom came to visit. She looked at the twisted, skeletal frame on the sofa, and compassion overcame her. She prayed, "Oh, Lord, why don't you heal this poor woman?"

The husband saw how deeply moved the visitor was, and he said, "God has a purpose in her sickness. Every other Christian in the city is watched closely by the secret police. But because she has been so sick for so long, no one ever looks in on her. They leave us alone, and she is the only person who can translate, undetected by the police."

It's inaccurate to say that God worked despite her weakness. The truth is that he was glorified through her weakness in a powerful way. You'd feel sorry for that woman, just as I would. But the very thing we'd wish and pray away, the very thing apparently destroying her life, the prickly thorn causing so much pain, was a holy place that allowed a very weak woman to become a pillar of strength in God's kingdom.[1]

My #1 Weakness (I Think)

I don't know what your weaknesses are. Actually, you may not be an expert on them either. I know I'm still figuring out all my own. Obviously we hide them from the world, but what's worse, we hide them from ourselves.

I have weaknesses devoted to hiding my weaknesses. My pride and my insecurity are involved in an ongoing conspiracy to cover up anything not in their interest. I realize that as a follower of Christ, I should delight in my deficiencies, knowing that they're mini-theaters open to the proclamation of the gospel.

Instead, my number one weakness is deliberately trying to be ignorant of my weaknesses. Quite honestly, I just don't want to know what they are because I'm afraid of vulnerability. (There's another one.) I want to sit with Stuart Smalley, the old *Saturday Night Live* character, and say, "I'm good enough, I'm smart enough, and dog-gone it, people like me!" But like him, I can't say any number of "daily affirmations" that will convince me.

In high school I was lifting weights at the gym with a good friend. He had just benched two hundred pounds. I had yet to approach that weight, but I was closing in, and if he could do it, so could I. Just not, you know, while people were watching.

So I waited until the gym was clear. I put the weight on the bar, and I did what I knew was the worst thing I could possibly do—the thing they teach you not to do when you lift weights: bench-press your maximum weight with no spotter present for safety purposes.

You're ready to fill in the conclusion of this story yourself. I can feel it. You're so certain that I couldn't lift the weight … that I tried lowering it back down and got trapped, and I called for help, and was all by myself … and then a big guy came back because he'd left his muscle oil … and he heard my cries and came sprinting in and rescued me from my plight … and that this big guy represents God in the story … and that my point is we should admit our weaknesses and cry out unto the Lord, and he'll come running to display his strength.

No. What actually happened was I lay down on the bench, gripped the bar, and prepared to lift. I felt the adrenaline kick in. I looked to my left. Then to my right. The stacks of weight looked like anvils. I got up, changed the weights back, and left the gym. I never told anyone about what I'd tried to do. More accurately, what I *thought* about trying to do. It wasn't because I was sure I couldn't lift it; it was because if I couldn't, I'd know I was weak, and I didn't want to know that. Ever since, I've wondered if I could have made that lift. I'll never know because of my fear of being weak and knowing it.

The weight room is one thing, and high school is one time. But I have to ask myself if it's part of a pattern. How many times as a pastor, as a husband, as a father, as a friend have I turned away from some challenge because I wasn't sure I had what it took and I was afraid to face the idea of weakness?

Christ is always moving us to press on toward the goal. He wants us to move on and to experience his blessings in our growth. How many blessings have I missed out on, not because I wasn't capable, but because I wasn't *vulnerable*? Rather than delighting in my weaknesses, I want to pretend they aren't there. Or at least be kind of fuzzy on their precise identities.

Paul started off that second letter to the Corinthians by reviewing the challenges he'd faced.

> We were under great pressure, far beyond our ability to endure. (1:8)

The lift was too imposing. His group was intimidated by the obstacle. They didn't have what it took because they were too weak. So they quit.

Actually, no.

> But this happened that we might not rely on ourselves but on God, who raises the dead. (v. 9)

Christ made the ultimate lift when he raised the dead. That's *power*. And he wants us to learn to trust his strength rather than our own. When we fail, when we're too weak, when we're at the end of ourselves, it's then that we have nowhere to go but to him. It's there where we discover his strength.

Our church staff sometimes studies books that will help us be more effective. A few years ago we read one called *Strengths Finder*. It included an online assessment that identified each person's top five strengths. It was helpful, clarifying who had which skills so we could better lean on one another. People like assessments, and a number of staff members printed out their top five strengths and posted them on their office doors.

All the while, however, I had an idea that wouldn't go away. Wouldn't it be even more helpful to work through a book called *Weaknesses Finder*? We wouldn't find that title, of course, because publishers would know they couldn't sell many copies of it. People like strengths. Weaknesses, not so much. But if God's strength shines in our weaknesses, shouldn't we want to post *those* on our doors?

The End of You

I guess it's just an eighty-two-year-old eccentric New Mexico multi-millionaire thing.

Forrest Fenn[†] filled a treasure chest with up to three million dollars in gold coins, diamonds, and emeralds and then buried it somewhere. Then he challenged America to go out and find it.

It all started when he was diagnosed with cancer in 1988. Fenn was going to bury the treasure and die out in the wilderness, leaving the hidden treasure as a legacy. He survived the cancer, but he moved forward with his treasure plans.

Fenn provided an unusual map to help people find the treasure: a poem with nine clues hidden in it. He could have gotten the idea from an old episode of *Scooby-Doo*. I don't know. But he has a very definite philosophy, and in his autobiography, *The Thrill of the Chase*, he laid it out for us. He wrote about the rare and valuable things he collected over the years, and how the real treasure in life is the pursuit itself.

By burying the treasure, he was trying to show as many people as possible what he meant. He was saying, "Turn off the TV! Get away

---

[†]   If that were your name, you'd have been an eccentric multimillionaire as well.

from those video games! Do something real for a change, instead of living vicariously on the adventures of fictional people on living room screens. Go after a true prize."

Fenn's message is that anything truly worth having must be pursued. You can own a DVD of *Treasure Island*, or you can get out of your recliner and live your own story, letting other people live vicariously through *your* adventures. The best stuff in life is buried. You have to go after it. You have to figure out where to dig, and then you have to go lay claim to it. Fenn believes it's high time people give up their tiny mass-market dreams and do something real and memorable.

You have to admit he has a compelling point. His challenge has inspired thousands of people to go in quest of his hidden treasure— which, so far, has eluded all pursuers. Every now and then he publishes a new "clue" based on undesired developments. It's not in a graveyard, so please don't dig those up. It's not at a historic landmark, so don't dig there either.

I suspect—because of the way most of us are wired—he touched a nerve. People believe there's something out there for them, but they can't seem to find it. Life itself is a kind of treasure hunt, and you have to think hard about what you're looking for and where to dig. And where do you find the map? In the movies, someone always finds an old treasure map, supposedly left by some pirate who opposed conventional banking, and the question is always whether the map is authentic.

A friend says, "This is it! This is the real map, and the treasure is on the island called Achievement." So you start out on your expedition, and it's hard walking, hard digging. After enough fifty- to sixty-hour workweeks, we find "it"—recognition, promotion, salary—and it doesn't really seem like much of a treasure.

Someone else is squinting at the map of the island of Wealth. Another believes the Love Boat will carry her to treasure buried on some island. The thrill of pursuit is nice, but you'd like to find a treasure that's ultimately worth something. And eventually you find yourself singing along with Bono, "I still haven't found what I'm looking for."

Death Is Life

The Bible says life's real prize is hidden, and you have to know where to search.

> For you died, and your life is now hidden with
> Christ in God. (Col. 3:3)

Paul says to live it you have to die first. In a gospel filled with paradoxes and "Wait, what?" statements, this is the ultimate one.

The end of me is where real life begins. And Jesus says that once I die, I can truly live.

Jesus closed the greatest sermon of all time by talking about two different paths—one leading to life and the other to destruction.

> Enter through the narrow gate. For wide is the gate
> and broad is the road that leads to destruction, and
> many enter through it. But small is the gate and
> narrow the road that leads to life, and only a few
> find it. (Matt. 7:13–14)

You can call it the first clue on the map Jesus leaves us. Look for a narrow gate. It won't be beautifully decorated or impressive. This gate is the kind most people ignore. But walk through it and the good times start coming, right? Wrong. You can expect a tough path, one seldom walked by others. It crosses through death but leads to life. Of all the upside-down teachings of Jesus, this is the greatest challenge to our sense of the world. As Bonhoeffer put it, when Christ calls someone, he bids them come and die.

Death is nobody's favorite word. We tiptoe around it with nicer names. Someone *passed on*. They've *gone ahead*. They *crossed the river*. They're *singing in the eternal choir*, because, you know, *God needed another angel*.

If polite, reverent euphemisms aren't our thing, we try to whistle past the graveyard with more jovial terms: *kicked the bucket; bought the farm; pushing up daisies*. Even *croaked*; *bit the big one; cashed in his chips*. We either oversoften the term or we make it into a joke—anything other than take it for what it is.

Beyond mere speech, we do everything we can to live in denial of the reality of death. We show the world a desperation to avoid it, as if nothing good could be waiting on the other side—or at the very least, as if we're not sure. It's not a very persuasive testimony for Christians to show the world, as we're dragged kicking and screaming to be with the one we've been worshipping all this time.

Even so, Jesus urges us to die. Not a physical death, of course—why not live to a ripe old age, move to Florida, and drive a Buick? No, Jesus speaks of dying to ourselves.

Our culture, of course, is all about celebrating ourselves, finding more life for ourselves. But no matter how hard we look, none of the maps lead there.

We spend years heading down the road of living for self instead of dying to it, and it's difficult to admit we've made the wrong choice. We've gone too many miles. We've invested too much in the journey. So we double down and step on the gas.

I hate admitting I've made the wrong journey. I've actually pulled up to the drive-through of a Chick-fil-A on Sunday, forgetting that the restaurant is closed on that day. Worse, I made the same mistake another time with my one of my daughters in the car. I got to the drive-through and felt silly. As we were leaving, another car replaced mine. My daughter said, "Are you going to remind them that the place is closed?"

No, I wasn't. That would have involved admitting I'd done the same thing, and I'm not too generous with my foul-ups. I'd rather bury those little treasures.

When we've chosen the wrong road, we don't like to acknowledge it to ourselves or to anyone else. Yet every now and then, we hear wealthy athletes, successful business people, and celebrated performers speak of struggling with depression and dealing with feelings of despair and worthlessness. We hear about a celebrity taking his own life, and just for a moment we wonder, have we been lied to? That was the fast lane, the one everyone wants to drive. He had money, she had fame—how can they not be living the life?

There are two different paths. One path is narrow, difficult, and marked "death," but it leads to life. The other path is broad, crowded, and marked "life," but it leads to death. In Matthew 16, Jesus tells us what we can expect when we follow him down the narrower road:

> Whoever wants to be my disciple must deny them-
> selves and take up their cross and follow me. For
> whoever wants to save their life will lose it, but who-
> ever loses their life for me will find it. (vv. 24–25)

How Dead People Think

How do we die to ourselves?

I've been around my share of dead people. I've been in the room before the coroner comes in. I've sat with families as their father and husband took his last breath. I've stood next to many open caskets as friends and family walked by to say good-bye. And I don't mean to be coarse, but I've noticed something about dead people.

They don't seem to care very much what other people think of them. They're not concerned with how nice their clothes are.

Dead people aren't caught up in their stock investments, nor do they show much interest in getting a promotion. Death renders all worldly points moot. It's the ultimate, required surrender of yourself and all you have. When Jesus speaks of dying to ourselves, this is what he wants us to think about. All the stuff of the world is dead to us, and we're dead to it.

This book has been a kind of path, a treasure hunt if you will, and on it we've followed Jesus through his teachings. We've seen how he turns the world's views inside out and upside down. He simply cuts against the grain of how we naturally think, and we realize that to follow Jesus, we need to retrain our minds to focus through spectacles we've never worn before. The key to thinking his way is an utter surrender, a giving up of the old ways, which never would have worked anyway.

It stumped the disciples too. On at least three different occasions, they got caught up in disputes over which one of them was the greatest. They were following a Teacher who taught them the last would be first and who showed them the model of a servant every day. But it was difficult to break loose from a lifetime of thought training. They tried to reconcile the kingdom of this world and the kingdom of God, which can't be done. Maybe that's been a challenge for you as you've made your way through this book. The journey to the end of me requires a completely different way of looking at this world. It's not natural and it doesn't come easily.

For the disciples, it ultimately came down to a question of life versus death. They had to decide if they were going to live for themselves or die to themselves. It's the same choice Jesus asks of you.

The softest bathrobe I ever wore was one offered by the Ritz-Carlton Hotel in Naples, Florida. I was officiating a wedding on the beach, and the bride and groom were kind enough to put us up there for the night. I had never expected to stay in such accommodations, and somehow that bathrobe symbolized the whole experience. To wear such a robe is to know that, if you're hungry, you need only pick up the phone and someone will bring you a very nice hamburger—though I always pictured the bathrobe set ordering lobster and filet mignon as a midnight snack. A sketchy-looking delivery boy, who may have sampled your food, doesn't bring it to the door; no, it's delivered by a gentleman in a tuxedo with a British accent. "Your cheeeese-buh-guh, suh."[†]

To wear such a robe means you can meander down to the spa and enjoy a relaxing massage. It means you suddenly think in terms of pampering yourself, taking care of *you*. By all means, toss your towels on the floor after your shower; the help will pick them up. And not only will they make your bed—they will leave chocolate on your pillow to thank you for letting them do it. People pay a premium to be pampered, to elevate the luxuries of the self.

Most of us would say, "That is the life." We want to be served. We want our every need met with tender loving care. It means you are successful and powerful. You've arrived. And as you read your map and choose your path, you deeply hope it will pass through the five-star hotels of the world.

But Jesus says that's not on the itinerary. Here, again, is the treasure quest he offers in that passage from Matthew 16:

1. Deny yourself.
2. Pick up your cross.
3. Follow him.
4. Prepare to die.

It's not the most enticing travel plan. But it's the reason the treasure is so elusive and so few seek it. You must enter the narrowest of

---

† Go ahead and say it out loud in your best British accent; you know you want to.

gates, travel the roughest of roads, and carry the cross on which you are prepared to die. And if you do all that, sincerely following the steps of Jesus, the craziest thing will happen; you will actually find the one true life. As I said earlier, the end of me is where real life begins.

Tale of the Towel

All through the Gospels, Jesus offers his life as a picture of his teaching. John 13 is among the most striking examples of what the end-of-me life looks like. It violates every tenet of the world's system. It involves service over rule, humility over pride—all the contradictions Jesus has been living and teaching us.

In this narrative, we step into the quiet upper room of a house where Jesus sits with his twelve disciples. It's past sundown on Thursday evening, and some of the men are still miffed over yet another argument over pecking order. Three years down the path, and they're still failing to understand the most central idea Jesus has been showing them.

Jesus declines to preach another sermon. What he does instead is shocking and distasteful to them. He picks up a towel and begins to wash feet. The most powerful teaching of all, of course, is Jesus living the life of utter humility rather than the way of a proud and influential rabbi.

The fact that the leader is serving his followers is odd enough, but it's actually a bit stranger than that. John tells us that Judas had already been tempted by the Devil to betray Jesus—to sell him out to the men who wanted him dead.

John also tells us that "Jesus knew that the Father had put all things under his power, and that he had come from God and was returning to God" (John 13:3).

In other words, Jesus fully understood his divine identity. He knew he was God, and he knew that all power in heaven and earth was his to command. And with this understanding, he allowed himself to be betrayed, to be taken, beaten, mocked, given a farce of a trial, and crucified. As he knew his status was the highest, he took up the lowest road, the most humble posture. He proceeded to wash the feet of a man who had arranged for his death.

As we step into this room, we know that Jesus is surrounded by men he loves and has molded and taught, and who will now abandon him at the first sign of danger. Judas will sell his whereabouts for a few coins. Peter will deny any knowledge of the man he has proclaimed is the Son of God. After three years of teaching multitudes, performing miracles, healing diseases, raising people from the dead, and bonding with his disciples, Jesus will proceed to his inglorious execution with only John and a few women still following. The rapturous crowds have vanished. The hour of the mockers and the bloodthirsty has arrived.

Jesus knew all this. You or I, with the same knowledge and the same power, probably would have run away. We might have leveraged some of that power against the forces set on killing us. At the very least, we might have given the disciples an earful.

But Jesus took a towel, dipped it in water, and continued to wash feet. The disciples were shocked, but not as much as they would have been if they had the full story, as we do. They didn't know about Judas. They didn't foresee the cross. Yet still, this scene was highly unsettling.

He got up from the meal, took off his outer clothing, and wrapped a towel around his waist. After
that, he poured water into a basin and began to
wash his disciples' feet, drying them with the towel
that was wrapped around him. (John 13:4–5)

Roads were dusty and eating was done on the floor. This made
foot washing an essential daily task. But it was a job reserved for
the lowest of servants. A slave would take care of it. It would have
been beneath the disciples, so none of them volunteered—certainly
not in the wake of an argument over who was the greatest and most
important among them.

There seemed to be no servants around. Maybe they would have
simply eaten with dirty, ugly feet in view—that would have been
preferable to a respectable person doing the washing. Yet Jesus knelt
and scrubbed away the grime.

Out of Line

God has a way of convicting us in terms of the subjects we
preach. I look at my topic for next Sunday and wonder what
difficult truth about myself God will lay on my heart. As I originally prepared to teach this one, I shouldn't have been surprised
by what happened. I was at the local pharmacy picking up a few
items, and I was second in line at the checkout counter. Three or
four customers got in line behind me. In my mind, I was moving
on to my next errands. Standing in line isn't one of my favorite
things.

But the woman in front of me was not only checking out using coupons—she was also paying by check. Impatient people notice things like that. *Personal check and coupons? I'll be here forever.*

Still, I caught myself. I wanted to focus on denying myself and serving others, in preparation for teaching John 13. I told God I wasn't falling for this one.

The coupons were processed, one by one. The woman began fishing around in her purse, looking for a pen so she could fill out the check. Once she got it, the pen was out of ink. As I watched her draw little circles on the back of her checkbook, trying to force the ink out, I broke into a cold sweat despite myself. *No, Lord,* I thought. *I won't be bothered by this.*

Then the cashier said, "I need to do a quick price check on this item. I think it just went on sale." A cold, clammy smile spread across my face. A gritted-teeth smile. *Being patient here. Just … dying to myself.*

When a voice then spoke, I thought it came from heaven: "I can check someone out in cosmetics," it said. Ah, deliverance. No doubt this was the reward of the Lord for my selfless spirit. I abruptly turned and headed toward cosmetics. God rewards the gentle and patient. *Good lesson to learn, Lord.*

Just as I reached the cosmetics counter, a man came huffing and puffing and shoving his cart from the back of our old line to the spot right in front of me. He was taking that "last shall be first" stuff pretty seriously.

Not only that, but I had two or three items—whereas this guy was unloading a full expedition of supplies on the counter from his shopping cart. "Who uses a cart at the drugstore? If you need a cart, go to Wal-Mart," I *thought* I sneered to myself inside my head. Did you note the little quotation marks around my statement? Those mean I said it out loud. I think in *italics*.

Yes, the man had heard me. He turned and gave me the look. I figured the worst thing would be for him to think I was a passive-aggressive wimp who said things under his breath, so I decided to be more direct. "I'm pretty sure I was next in line, buddy."

I hope that didn't come across in print as if I hissed it through clenched teeth, because I didn't. No, I had a nice, neighborly smile on my face. Except I used the word *buddy*. No matter how much you smile, that one always sounds like a curse word. So once again, I tried to overcompensate for things by talking. That's how preachers handle things, you understand—this situation could use more talking. "You're pretty fast with that cart," I said. "I didn't realize I should stretch out before coming to Walgreens." I gave a fake laugh.

He never said a word, but now all his stuff was unloaded on the counter.

I looked back at the first line I was in, which was now flowing like promises at a political convention. The check-and-coupon lady was long since gone, and people were moving through at a good clip. *I'd be driving home, enjoying my candy bar by now if I hadn't changed lines.*[†]

[†]   I always choose the wrong line. When choosing a line, I will sometimes say to myself, *Normally I would choose line #1 but I know I always choose the wrong line, so I will go with line #2.* Inevitably line #2 ends up being longer. So the next time I will say to myself, *Normally I would choose line #1 and then decide to go with line #2 since I always choose the wrong line only to discover that line #2 is longer, so I will choose line #1.* But it's difficult to beat God at the "which of the three bowls is the marble under" game. I always lose.

The man with the cart looked at me and said, "I was in a hurry." It wasn't exactly an apology, and as I looked at his goods, I thought, *No one in a hurry buys a dancing Santa Claus.*

I said, "Well, you sure got over here in a hurry."

He said, "Well, I have lung cancer." It may sound contrived, but that's exactly what he said. He played the cancer card. I guess it's a trump card for any tense situation, even if it's said with an attitude.

At this point, of course, my heart should have been softened. Of course I should have remembered my intent to deny myself and live as a servant of others. Of course I should have expressed sympathy and offered prayer. Of course. Instead, I'm pretty sure I rolled my eyes while breathing heavily and rapidly through my nose.

As I was finally being checked out, "O Holy Night," sung by Harry Connick Jr., played over the speakers in the store. The third verse rang loud and clear: "Truly he taught us to love one another; his law is love, and his gospel is peace."

Compounded Daily

Each day is a new narrow gate. The problem with dying to myself is that it's so daily. I have to make the choice over and over again. I can live for myself or I can live for Christ, which means picking up my cross—at the drugstore, at the gas pump, in my living room, in traffic.

Not only must I serve the people I love and admire, and those who can make my life easier, but dying to myself also means serving those I don't really like or understand and even those who have hurt me. How can you serve a husband who is apathetic rather than loving? A wife who never speaks an encouraging word? A child bent on rebellion? How do you serve the coworker who talked behind your back? The rude guy across the street? The driver who takes your life into his hands on the highway? It takes dying to yourself. If Jesus can wash the feet of Judas, then it's time for me to come to the end of myself and follow his example.

The Ritz-bathrobe life appeals to us because it's just us and those who serve us. The towel-and-water life is the mirror image of that, and it doesn't appeal to us. "Why should I do this?" we ask. "Somebody should serve me just once. Don't I do more than my part? Why can't I have it as easy as some people I could name?"

And as we sulk in our entitlement, we look down to see Jesus scrubbing our feet—Jesus, who is perfect and receives as his reward the worst abuse men could offer. Jesus, God in flesh, who humbled himself and took the form of a servant; Jesus, who gives to us so much, his very life, knowing that we could offer him nothing in return.

Jesus hung on the cross and interceded before God for the men who crucified him. As he bled and slowly suffocated, he asked God to forgive his executioners, for they didn't really understand their actions.

Jesus was at the end of his ministry, the end of his earthly life, the end of himself, but he knew he was at the beginning of something that changed everything. At the end of death and suffering and sacrifice comes the beginning of Resurrection.

In order to serve those it's hardest to serve, you must die to yourself. And you'll find the most surprising and transforming blessing as you forgive those who have hurt you. To betray your bitterness and anger by flying in its face, by acting counter to it, is to escape its miserable grip on your life. It is to release yourself from a self-imposed prison sentence.

Back in that room, Jesus washed feet at the very moment when he might have been caught up in his own problems. When life isn't going well, you want to put on the bathrobe, eat some comfort food, and "have some time to yourself." When we're troubled, we do exactly the wrong thing.

Self-absorption is poor medicine. Tough times don't feel natural for serving others, but it's amazing how healing it is to go serve someone else. Sure, you have friends who would probably come, pamper you, and serve you while you brood. But Jesus did precisely the opposite of asking to be pampered. He pampered others. Perhaps he strengthened himself for the nightmare to come by taking the towel rather than the bathrobe.

The healthiest thing you can do in rugged waters is to serve someone else.

Even at Christmas, the time when we celebrate the humility of the manger, we make the holiday into a time to be served rather than to serve. As I write these words, the gifts are wrapped beneath our tree. Over the years I've noticed that our children count the boxes. And not only do they count their own gifts; they count their siblings' gifts to make sure no one is getting more than they are. When they're younger, the kids also pay attention to who gets the largest packages. We say, "Well, thank goodness they grow up," but I'm not so sure we do. We simply hide it better. We tell our spouse, "You really don't need to get me anything this year." Those experienced in marriage know to disregard that sentiment. What it really means is, "I want you to know I'm not the demanding type. But if you fail to get me something, I'll hold it over you until the day you die!"

It's inherently human to focus on ourselves. It's how we are. Jesus teaches us to deny ourselves, to die to ourselves, but that doesn't mean it ever becomes easy. Each day when we climb out of bed to begin a new day, we're still human. The old self gets out of bed with us, and we have to put on Christ as an act of will, over and over.

From Now On

Jesus finishes his work and tells the disciples that, now that he has done it, they should wash one another's feet (John 13:14). The verb for *wash* indicates ongoing and continual action. Jesus isn't saying to do this as an exercise today. He's saying to do it from now on. They've been bickering over their ranking, and Jesus tells them to humble themselves, each below the other, from now on. He calls them to come to the end of themselves every day and in every relationship.

The time for themselves was all about the bathrobe—self-promotion, ladder climbing, competition.

The end of themselves was about the towel—service, encouragement, blessing others. Death.

The paradox, of course, is that Jesus says it is death that leads the way to life. How can that be? I can learn what it means only by doing what it demands. When I come to the end of me, when I deny myself, I begin to feel free from that ceaseless struggle expressed by the disciples and their cartoonish quarreling. I am freed from the tyranny and loneliness of self-absorption. I have died to that, and now I can live for Christ.

You could keep doing life the old way, trying to climb, trying to possess, trying to gain. Jesus would then ask this question: "What good will it be for someone to gain the whole world, yet forfeit their soul?" (Matt. 16:26). In other words, what if you actually catch what you're chasing? What if you get the ultimate mansion, the corner office, the limited-edition Mercedes? What if the buried treasure is an empty box? What if you realize you've lost your soul somewhere in the relentless pace?

The Poseidon Adventure is a movie about an ocean liner that hits a terrible storm. A wall of water crashes through the ballroom. Men in tuxes and women in evening gowns are screaming and running for cover. Amid all the confusion, after the lights go out, the ship flips over.

There is enough air trapped inside to keep the liner floating upside down. But the passengers are in full panic, frantically trying to save their own lives. They're so confused that they begin climbing the stairs to the top deck. The problem is that this deck is now one hundred feet underwater. Getting to the "top" of the ship means drowning.

The only survivors are those who challenge the old, established logic of up and down. While others rush to their doom, these wiser passengers descend into the dark belly of the ship until they reach the hull. At the bottom of the ship they find the surface of the ocean— that is, the top. Rescuers hear them banging at the hull, and they cut them free.

The ship of this world has turned upside down, so that what looks like up to us is really the way to destruction; what seems like down to us is the way to salvation.

Only if we follow Jesus, only if we choose the way of the cross and denial of self, can we truly live.

The End of Me

I want to challenge you to look around—at home, at work, and where you live—and find ways to set aside the bathrobe and pick up the towel. Dying to myself and reaching the end of me is meant to be a daily decision *and* a daily demonstration.

As a pastor and an author, I sometimes end up using especially dramatic examples as a way to inspire, and frankly I'm doing my best to keep your attention. But what makes Jesus's example of washing feet so powerful is that it was a simple demonstration. When you come to the end of yourself, you are no longer concerned with the big deal or the dramatic demonstration.

I want to leave you with a simple example of what I'm talking about in hopes that it will inspire other such stories. Nothing over the top or melodramatic. This one came across my desk this week. Jack and Patsy Riley attend the church where I preach, and they're successful business owners, well-respected in our community.

You might expect them to live in a luxurious home. Yet they live in what some would call a rough neighborhood. On a number of occasions, they've considered moving. But, for one thing, they want to be close to their parents. Plus, they've usually been too busy to think about house hunting anyway.

One weekend at church, the Rileys heard a sermon about showing the love of Jesus to people in the community by reaching out to those in need. As always, the couple took that message to heart. Patsy decided that God was calling her to get to know single mothers and seniors in her neighborhood so she could be a better servant to them. She threw an old-fashioned block party, with popcorn, hot dogs, and lemonade. The Rileys distributed 150 fliers door to door. On the day of the party, people filled every square foot of their yard, laughing, having fun, and building relationships.

Across the street is an Economy Inn. Patsy looked up and noticed there were people on the balcony, watching the party. Immediately she felt the conviction that the Spirit of God was saying, *This is your time to do something.* The Economy Inn provides low-income housing, and she decided to throw a Christmas party for the residents.

They chose the date of December 15 and started to plan. They bought refreshments, put up a nativity set, purchased Wal-Mart gift cards, and set up games for the children. More than one hundred residents from across the street came to the Rileys' party. There were college students who needed to live close to the bus line, families who had lost their homes, and seniors who had lived at the Economy Inn for years.

The guests enjoyed a feast of lasagna, bread, salad, and desserts of every kind. Patsy also handed out small containers so people could take leftovers home with them. New friendships were made by the dozens that day. The laughter was pure and authentic, in keeping with the joy people feel when something truly good is happening and the cynicism and small-mindedness of our time is shut out for an evening.

It was a stretch for Jack and Patsy to pull off these events. They gave of their time, their talents, their money, their energy. They set aside personal ambitions, set their "self" aside, and simply served and gave. What they got in return was far more than they sacrificed.

If you'd been there, you might have wondered why we can't live more like this every day. It's not as if this was such a rare and precious opportunity. But the reality is, if we were to ask God to put us to work, as the Rileys did, he would begin pointing out places right and left for us to spring into action. Those places are everywhere. Denying ourselves—or, said another way, loving others—isn't an occasional option; it's a way of life that casts its influence over every day. It's God's way of ushering in his kingdom, house by house, Walgreens by Walgreens, face by face, moment by moment.

This is the death we must die. Not a one-time death. Not a partial death. It's a daily dying. And every time I come to the end of me, I discover what I deeply wanted all along—real and abundant life in Christ.

Challenge Questions

Chapter 1

1. Think of a time in your life when you knew Jesus was real and present. Then write out your own conclusion to this sentence: Jesus became real when …

2. What does "bankrupt in spirit" mean to you? When have you experienced it?

3. How would you describe the blessing that follows being poor in spirit?

Chapter 2

1. In what ways do you avoid being seen as broken?

2. When in your life have you experienced mourning? How would you describe the blessing that resulted from it?

3. If you're unable to see the blessing that comes with mourning, how might you embrace the pain?

Chapter 3

1. Have you experienced the blessing of facing up to sin? If so, how did you feel?

2. In what ways have you caught yourself behaving like a Pharisee? Be honest! Remember, it's always the truth that will set you free.

3. In what ways do you take ownership of your own humility?

Chapter 4

1. In your own words, how would you describe having a pure heart?

2. In what ways are you sometimes inauthentic with others?

3. Think of a time when you confessed a sin to God and/or another person. How did you feel afterward?

Chapter 5

1. When in your life have you experienced emptiness?

2. In what ways has God shown up to fill your emptiness?

3. What people, places, or activities take up the space in your life that is meant for God? Are you willing to give those to him?

Chapter 6

1. Is there an area or a circumstance in your life that has you feeling helpless? I challenge you right now to take an action—pray, talk to someone, make a decision … take up your mat and walk—take an action that will empower you. If you're not sure what to do, ask God, listen, then do what he tells you to do.

2. What gets in your way of asking for help? Are you willing to give that up and let God or another person help you?

3. What are your thoughts on the idea that the more helpless you are, the better?

Chapter 7

1. If money and time were no issue, what would you want God to use you for?

2. What are the things that make you feel disqualified to serve God? Who said those things are true?

3. Make a list of all your "disqualifications." Then surrender them, renounce them, and tear up the paper you wrote them on.

Chapter 8

1. What are the weaknesses in your life?

2. How have you noticed God's strength in spite of your weaknesses?

3. In what ways do you tend to hide your weaknesses? What would happen if you exposed them?

The End of You

1. Read Matthew 7:13–14 again. How often to you find yourself wandering down the broad road? What do you do to get back on the narrow road?

2. Read Matthew 16:24–25 again. How often do you catch yourself trying to save your own life?

3. Getting to the end of yourself means you lose your life (your ego, your survival tactics) for Jesus. It means you die every day as you intentionally choose the upside-down ways of Jesus. Are you ready to go for it?

I'd love to hear how it goes for you, so please write to me via Facebook: www.facebook.com/kyleidleman

Or through my website: www.kyleidleman.com

Notes

Chapter 1: Broken to Be Whole

1. "Evolution of Dance," YouTube video, 6:00, posted by Judson Laipply, April 6, 2006, www.youtube.com/watch?v=dMH0bHeiRNg.
2. "Teaser of the Upcoming Documentary Film *Landfill Harmonic*," YouTube video, 3:27, posted by LandfillHarmonic, November 17, 2012, www.youtube.com/watch?v=fXynrsrTKbI.
3. Brené Brown, *I Thought It Was Just Me (But It Isn't)* (New York: Gotham, 2007), 145.

Chapter 2: Mourn to Be Happy

1. William Barclay, *The Gospel of Matthew*, vol. 1 (Louisville, KY: Westminster John Knox Press, 2001), 107.
2. Saint Augustine, *Confessions*, vol. 5 (UK: Penguin, 2003), 103.

Chapter 3: Humbled to Be Exalted

1. Warren W. Wiersbe, *Wiersbe's Expository Outlines on the New Testament* (Colorado Springs, CO: David C Cook, 1992), 83.
2. Nik Wallenda with David Ritz, *Balance: A Story of Faith, Family, and Life on the Line* (New York: FaithWords, 2013), 207–8.

Chapter 4: Authentic to Be Accepted

1. John R. W. Stott, *The Message of the Sermon on the Mount* (Downers Grove, IL: InterVarsity Press, 1985), 49.

Chapter 5: Empty to Be Filled

1. Mother Teresa of Calcutta, *Life in the Spirit: Reflections, Meditations, Prayers*, ed. Kathryn Spink (San Francisco: HarperCollins, 1983), 31.
2. Tim Kreider, "The 'Busy' Trap," *The Opinion Pages* (blog), *New York Times*, June 30, 2012, , http://opinionator.blogs.nytimes.com/2012/06/30/the -busy-trap/?_r=0.
3. Tiffany Limtanakool, "TV-Turnoff Week Promotes Healthy Living," Medscape, www.medscape.com/viewarticle/503758.
4. Quentin Hardy, "The Rise of the Toilet Texter," *Bits* (blog), *New York Times*, January 30, 2012, http://bits.blogs.nytimes.com/2012/01/30 /the-rise-of-the-toilet-texter/.
5. Gary Thomas, *The Sacred Search: What If It's Not about Who You Marry, But Why?* (Colorado Springs, CO: David C Cook, 2013) 29–30.
6. D. L. Moody, quoted in Josiah Hotchkiss Gilbert, *Dictionary of Burning Words of Brilliant Writers: A Cyclopedia of Quotations from the Literature of All Ages* (New York: Wilbur B. Ketcham, 1895), 319.
7. D. L. Moody, quoted in Martin H. Manser, comp., *The Westminster Collection of Christian Quotations: Over 6,000 Quotations Arranged by Theme* (Louisville, KY: Westminster John Knox Press, 2001), 47.

Chapter 6: Helpless to Be Empowered

1. Michael E. Addis and James R. Mahalik, "Men, Masculinity, and the Contexts of Help Seeking," *American Psychologist*, January 2003, 5.
2. Frank Minirth and Paul Meier, *Happiness Is a Choice: New Ways to Enhance Joy and Meaning in Your Life* (Grand Rapids, MI: Baker Books, 2013), 126.

Chapter 7: Disqualified to Be Chosen

1. Chuck Colson, "God Used My Greatest Defeat," sermon illustration, taken from the sermon "The Gravy Train Gospel," *PreachingToday*, accessed December 18, 2014, www.preachingtoday.com/illustrations/2012/may /7050712.html.

Chapter 8: Weak to Be Strong

1. Corrie ten Boom, *Tramp for the Lord: The Story that Begins Where The Hiding Place Ends* (Fort Washington, PA: CLC Publications, 2011), 187–89.

Take a 40-Day Journey to Lasting Transformation

Do you want to see change in your life but don't know how to make it happen? In this thoughtful devotional, Kyle Idleman shares three key elements—Awakening, Honesty, and Action—that will challenge you to work through the circumstance or thought pattern that is preventing you from moving forward.

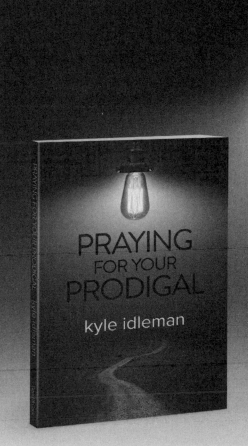

PRAYING
FOR YOUR
PRODIGAL

kyle idleman

Hope for
the Prodigals
and Those
Who Love
Them

A book for parents and family members of those who are far from God, *Praying for Your Prodigal* combines letters from parents to their wandering child, specific prayers to pray through, and insights from the parable of the prodigal son. This promise-filled book reminds you that you are not alone and reveals new ways you can love your prodigal as he or she is loved by God.

the lightbulb just went on

We've all had "aha moments" in our lives, insights that change everything. With everyday examples and trademark testimonies, bestselling author Kyle Idleman of *Not a Fan* draws on Scripture to reveal how three key elements— ***Awakening, Honesty, Action***—can produce the same kind of "aha!" in our spiritual lives.